Women of Achievement

Ellen DeGeneres

Women *of* Achievement

Susan B. Anthony

Hillary Rodham Clinton

Marie Curie

Ellen DeGeneres

Nancy Pelosi

Rachael Ray

Eleanor Roosevelt

Martha Stewart

Women of Achievement

Ellen DeGeneres

ENTERTAINER

Sherry Beck Paprocki

CHELSEA HOUSE
PUBLISHERS
An imprint of Infobase Publishing

ELLEN DeGENERES

Chelsea House
An imprint of Infobase Publishing
132 West 31st Street
New York NY 10001

Library of Congress Cataloging-in-Publication Data

Paprocki, Sherry Beck.
  Ellen DeGeneres : Entertainer / Sherry Beck Paprocki.
    p. cm. — (Women of achievement)
  Includes bibliographical references and index.
  ISBN 978-1-60413-082-9 (hardcover)
  1. DeGeneres, Ellen. 2. Comedians—United States—Biography. 3. Television personalities—United States—Biography. I. Title. II. Series.

  PN2287.D358P37 2009
  792.702'8092—dc22
  [B]

                              2008034638

Chelsea House books are available at special discounts when purchased in bulk quantities for businesses, associations, institutions, or sales promotions. Please call our Special Sales Department in New York at (212) 967-8800 or (800) 322-8755.

You can find Chelsea House on the World Wide Web at http://www.chelseahouse.com

Series design by Erik Lindstrom
Cover design by Ben Peterson

Printed in the United States of America

Bang EJB 10 9 8 7 6 5 4 3 2 1

This book is printed on acid-free paper.

All links and Web addresses were checked and verified to be correct at the time of publication. Because of the dynamic nature of the Web, some addresses and links may have changed since publication and may no longer be valid.

CONTENTS

She's a
Dancing Machine

The music is blaring out over *The Ellen DeGeneres Show* as the host does her famous dance moves onstage. The entire audience stands up to dance with her, and she doesn't miss a beat. In her trademark Vans and black slacks, Ellen DeGeneres makes dancing look easy. But for DeGeneres, one of the first really famous female comedians, it has taken years to get to the point where she can strut her carefree moves in front of a packed audience. Once the music stops on this December day, wild applause follows.

It is the end of 2007, and the fun on the show has just begun. During this episode, world-renowned chef Wolfgang Puck will fry some mini-hamburgers and teach DeGeneres to make quesadillas. In a holiday mood, the show's host will thrill audience members when she gives them beds, sheets,

Ellen DeGeneres danced as Kanye West performed during a special taping of an outdoor episode of DeGeneres's talk show. The taping took place in May 2006 at Johnny Carson Park in Burbank, California. Dancing has become a signature of DeGeneres's daytime talk show.

blankets, and other items. She will interview a photographer who has produced a book about wild animals, and she will introduce 15-year-old singer Charice Pempengco from the Philippines, whose video she spotted on YouTube. Still, that's not all. DeGeneres will also give away hundreds of dollars to a woman in the audience selected to step into the phone-booth-size "gold digger" machine. And, of course, DeGeneres will dance to the rap song of the same name while the woman frantically grabs for money as it blows around inside the machine.

DeGeneres has figured out a way to entertain a wide audience. Her hourlong show is lively. Each day, she offers a blur of activities that seems to go unmatched by other daytime talk-show hosts, moving swiftly from one topic to the next. Her trademark humor is found not just from the words she chooses but also from the way she says them. As photographer Andrew Zuckerman talks about his book on her show, she comes across a picture of Zuckerman being lifted high off the ground by an elephant's trunk. "Is this something that went terribly wrong, or what?" she deadpans as Zuckerman and the audience break out in laughter.

A lifelong animal lover, DeGeneres has openly discussed her pets and other animals during her career. In the fall of 2007, she made national headlines when a dog adoption went afoul. The dog, named Iggy, was adopted by DeGeneres, who then gave it to her hairdresser's family after the dog had trouble getting along with DeGeneres's cats. The rescue organization, however, insisted that Iggy be returned because the hairdresser's family was not approved for adoption. The incident so upset DeGeneres that she cried while offering an apology on her show. "I feel totally responsible for it, and I'm so sorry," she sobbed. "I'm begging them (the rescue organization) to give that dog back to that family. I just want the family to have their dog."[1]

This was a rare day on DeGeneres's show. Certainly, the comedian is better known for making people laugh than for crying.

CREATING HER OWN PATH

DeGeneres followed no formula to get to this point in life—to being a funny woman with a stage on which to

ELLEN'S DJ, TONY OKUNGBOWA

When Ellen DeGeneres wants to move and shake, it's DJ Tony Okungbowa who plays the tunes. For several years, Okungbowa has been DeGeneres's main sidekick on her talk show. He first appeared soon after *The Ellen DeGeneres Show* debuted in 2003, and he continued until 2006. After taking a few years off to pursue his passion for acting, he was back for the 2008–2009 season.

Okungbowa was born in Nigeria and lived in London, Nigeria, and New York as he was growing up. The middle of seven children, he became a DJ at 18. He moved to New York in the 1990s to pursue a career in acting. Later, while living in Los Angeles, he and a photographer friend, Andrew McPhearson, developed an idea. Okungbowa would play music while McPhearson did photo shoots of celebrities for publications like *TV Guide* and *Glamour*. Okungbowa met DeGeneres during a shoot for *TV Guide*, and a few days later she invited him to join her on the show.

Back then, no one was sure that a DJ on a daytime talk show would work. As it turned out, Okungbowa's selection of popular hits led DeGeneres to dance more and more with each show. Thanks to him, the DJ format has become a huge hit. In those early years, after DeGeneres delivered her monologue at the beginning of the show, she would say, "Tony, make me dance." And, he would.* In the process, Okungbowa started to become a celebrity, too.

entertain five days a week. There is no college degree that made her comedy career happen. Certainly, there were only a few role models to follow. Before DeGeneres, the number

Despite his success during those first three seasons, Okungbowa had other passions. He was eager to return to acting and decided he would leave the show. When he wrapped up the 2005–2006 season, he was surprised with a visit from The Pussycat Dolls, who performed on the show. And he received a Cartier watch as DeGeneres and her staff wished him well. Audience members were happy, too, when each person received two roundtrip tickets to London on Virgin Atlantic Airlines.

As an actor, Okungbowa has appeared on episodes of *Law & Order: SVU*, *The X Files*, *NYPD Blue*, and other programs. He also released a compilation of his favorite songs, called *Hollywood Sessions*. But he missed the DeGeneres show and decided to return after his two-year hiatus.

Okungbowa came back with his trademark high energy and infectious laugh, ready to rock with DeGeneres on one of television's most popular daytime talk shows. Okungbowa's job also involves selecting the appropriate music to play when guests walk out and during other times of the hour-long program. Besides spinning music, he banters with DeGeneres about pop culture and current events. The two have a fun rapport. When she tells jokes, it's not unusual for him to toss in a few punch lines of his own, delivered in his British accent.

*Lola Ogunnaike, "He Toils, He Spins (on Daytime TV), He Makes 'Ellen' Boogie." *The New York Times*, February 7, 2005.

of female comedians was slim, among them Phyllis Diller, Joan Rivers, and Roseanne Barr. DeGeneres's career in comedy has come from a lot of hard work, some bad experiences, and a bit of good luck.

Through the years, television and newspaper critics have said that DeGeneres has a distinctive way of telling funny stories. She has the uncanny ability to use a technique called the pregnant pause—which gives the audience time to understand a joke and to laugh at it. They also say that her observational humor—her insight into how people act—is among the best in the business. And even though DeGeneres is a woman, she has avoided the trap that has befallen other female comedians—humor that focuses only on being a woman isn't part of her comedy routine.[2]

"I have never in my comedy done 'female humor,'" she told a reporter for *The Washington Post* in 1994. "I have a mixture in my audience of everybody—young and old, black and white, male and female. And that's how I want my audience to be."[3]

DeGeneres credits male comedians, including Bob Newhart, Woody Allen, and Steve Martin, for influencing her. When her first television show appeared in the early 1990s, she was often compared with the famed Jerry Seinfeld. DeGeneres's show, initially called *These Friends of Mine*, had a cast in their late 20s and early 30s similar to the cast on Seinfeld's show. While Seinfeld's main cast of characters involved three men and a woman, *These Friends of Mine* featured three women and a man. DeGeneres, though, says that it's unfair to compare comedians with one another. "I always tried to be myself," she once told Larry King on his CNN talk show. "And the reason people are successful is they're unique."[4]

LAUGHTER AND TEARS

Unique, indeed, is one way to describe DeGeneres. She grew up in a not-so-well-off family in New Orleans, and her parents divorced when she was a teenager. During high school, she moved to a small town in Texas because her mother, Betty, had remarried.[5] Betty fell ill with breast cancer and had a mastectomy, causing more stress in DeGeneres's young life.[6] It seems, however, that during times of hardship, DeGeneres's humor comes through. Back in the 1970s, she spent hours making her mother laugh so hard that she cried; then DeGeneres would mimic her mother crying, and they would laugh really hard all over again.

Even though she focused on cheering up her mother during her fight against cancer, not everything in DeGeneres's life was funny. She says she was sexually abused by her stepfather as a teenager but kept the secret from her mother while Betty DeGeneres recovered from cancer.[7] When DeGeneres was 20, she told her mother that she was a lesbian, but she kept quiet about her personal life for many years during her burgeoning career—until she made a very public announcement.[8]

DeGeneres's goal to be a comedian was a huge challenge. After graduating from high school, she attended college briefly, dropping out within a few months. She worked a multitude of jobs—waiting tables, selling vacuum cleaners, painting houses, washing cars, checking gloves as they were being made in a factory, and working for a law firm. Her friends thought she was funny, but she was not outgoing or particularly popular. Yet, at some point she decided that she would try to make a living out of being funny, and she set out to accomplish that goal.

THE FUNNIEST PERSON IN AMERICA

While working at the law firm, DeGeneres focused on her stand-up comedy by performing at local clubs in New Orleans. Her videotaped performances led her to win the title of Showtime's Funniest Person in America in 1982. "I never fit in at the law firm," she told a reporter at the *Detroit*

Free Press more than 10 years later. "It was too serious, and I never liked being told what to do."[9]

Although the title may have launched a successful career, DeGeneres claimed that being deemed America's funniest person caused a lot of stress. The job involved touring the country for the next year and appearing at some unusual stops. "I was traveling around and somebody would see the funniest person in America is appearing at Chuckles and you know, the mini-mall. And they'd walk in and of course be dis-appointed," she told Larry King during a 2004 interview.[10]

As always, DeGeneres worries about disappointing people. Her self-effacing humor has caused fans to laugh for many years, though, so it seems that she has become comfortable with her role in life. Her early comedy covered topics like animals, her fear of flying, and the strange things that people do. "People are stupid," she once told a crowd back in 1984. "Ever notice when you're with someone and they have something that tastes bad, they ask you to taste it? And we do."[11]

DeGeneres's success, though, has not been without setbacks. Her public announcement that she was gay in 1997—nearly two decades after she shared that information with her mother—was blamed for the eventual cancellation of her first television sitcom. Years of little work followed, and she thought her career as a comedian might be over. Yet, DeGeneres relied on her ability to make people laugh to help her through this difficult situation, too. Her sense of humor was apparent during interviews with talk-show hosts. She appeared on *Larry King Live*, *Late Night with Conan O'Brien*, *The Rosie O'Donnell Show*, and Howard Stern's radio program. In addition, she produced some comedy specials with HBO. "Ellen is one of the few pre-mier comics, and she has a great sense on the stand-up stage of what works for her," an HBO executive, Carolyn Strauss, once told a reporter for the *Los Angeles Daily News*.[12]

During the time that her television career was slow, she also did the voice-over for a friendly fish named Dory in the animated film *Finding Nemo*. The story of how she became the voice of Dory matches much about DeGeneres's career: She was in the right place at the right time. She once told Larry King that the writer of *Finding Nemo*, Andrew Stanton, overheard her voice as his wife was watching the *Ellen* show and he wrote the dialogue for the rambling fish Dory with DeGeneres in mind.[13]

Finding Nemo was soon followed by the debut and quick success of her daytime talk show. Today, DeGeneres's show has a widely diverse audience, and she's watched by millions of people every day. Her popularity, too, has made her a financial success. *Forbes* magazine estimates her personal fortune at $65 million. In 2007, *Forbes* placed her fifteenth on a list called "The Forbes TV 20," which featured the top-earning television celebrities.[14] The magazine said that DeGeneres was earning $15 million a year for work that included her syndicated talk show. *Forbes* also listed DeGeneres as one of the "20 Richest Women in Entertainment." She was the only comedian on the list.[15]

Since her very public coming out, DeGeneres has been fairly quiet regarding her sexuality. Yet her stance has perhaps made the topic of homosexuality more mainstream today. On her television show, DeGeneres seems like the friend everyone loves. She gets rave reviews from people as young as grade-schoolers and as old as great-grandparents.

AN IMPORTANT 'PHONE CALL'

One of DeGeneres's first stand-up monologues, involving a conversation with God, was a result of her grief after the death of a close friend in her early 20s. The friend, who had been DeGeneres's roommate, died in an automobile accident. DeGeneres recalled her sadness when a writer from *The New York Times* interviewed her. After her friend's

Ellen DeGeneres is shown during a performance on *The Tonight Show* in February 1987. She made her debut on Johnny Carson's late-night talk show the year before, performing her "conversation with God" monologue. Afterward, Carson invited DeGeneres over to chat with him. She was the first female comedian ever to receive such an invitation in her first appearance on the program.

death, DeGeneres was forced to move to a cheap apartment that had fleas, but comedy sparked in her mind one evening while trying to go to sleep. "So I started writing what it would be like to call God and ask why fleas are here and this person is not," she recalled. "But my mind just kicked into what all of a sudden would happen if you actually picked up the phone and called God. How it would take forever, how it would ring for a long time because . . . it's a big place."[16]

Six years later, DeGeneres used that conversation with God when she appeared on Johnny Carson's late-night talk show. After her monologue, Carson invited her to come over to the sofa and talk with him. Carson rarely did that—DeGeneres was the first and only woman comic ever to be asked over to the sofa in her first appearance on *The Tonight Show*. The invitation, however, was one that DeGeneres says she had imagined years before. And it was an invitation that launched her career.

A Broken Home

Ellen Lee DeGeneres was late—she was born two weeks after her mother expected her arrival. Finally, on January 26, 1958, she was born at Ochsner Foundation Hospital, which still exists near New Orleans in Jefferson Parish, Louisiana. DeGeneres was a large baby, weighing nine pounds, thirteen ounces.[1] Vance, her brother, was nearly three-and-a-half years old at the time.

In the beginning, DeGeneres's paternal grandmother, whom she and Vance called Mumsy, also lived with the family in a house that had two bedrooms and one bath. They lived in a town near New Orleans called Metairie. DeGeneres's mother, Betty, says that some of the happiest times of her life were when her children were growing up and she was spending a lot of time with them. Betty

DeGeneres and Ellen's father, Elliott, had various jobs, but eventually her father started to sell insurance.

The DeGeneres family belonged to a religion called Christian Science, and they attended Sunday school on a regular basis. DeGeneres's parents were quite religious when she was a child, and the DeGeneres family would be considered normal in nearly every way. DeGeneres's father had a keen sense of humor, and the entire family enjoyed his spontaneity. "We joked and laughed a lot," Betty DeGeneres wrote in her book, *Love, Ellen*.[2] She says that Ellen's and Vance's abilities to develop their humor have contributed to the success they have had as adults.

"As a little girl, she made me laugh," DeGeneres's mother once told a reporter from *In Style* magazine. "She was a great child, always very caring, loved animals, always rescuing baby birds and kittens. . . . She's a good soul."[3] Ellen once recalled carrying around a doll called Baby Dear. "My brother, Vance, cut her hair," she said.[4]

There is no doubt that Ellen loved animals. Her family had a pet parakeet that flew away never to be found. They also had other pets, such as fish and dogs. Ellen brought home a lot of stray animals, including dogs, birds, a cat, and even a snake one time. Ellen's early love of animals has led to her lifelong commitment to rescuing pets from animal shelters and giving them good homes—with either herself or other people she knows.

THE ROCK 'N' ROLL GENERATION

Ellen and Vance were like many other children of the time, showing a lot of enthusiasm for rock music when one of the first prominent rock-and-roll bands, The Beatles, started to perform in the United States in the mid-1960s. The DeGeneres family liked to watch a television variety program called *The Ed Sullivan Show*, on

Rock-and-roll was a new sound in the early 1960s, and like many other youngsters back then, Ellen DeGeneres and her brother, Vance, were big fans. The band that perhaps had the biggest impact was The Beatles. Here, the British band makes its historic U.S. debut on February 9, 1964, on *The Ed Sullivan Show*.

which The Beatles first performed, as well as other similar shows. Betty DeGeneres worried that her children spent too much time watching television. Now she realizes that those early shows may have helped them prepare for their careers. Both eventually became involved in the entertainment industry.

Vance still remembers the first time he saw The Beatles. He was 10 years old and was watching the same show that millions of children and adults across the country were watching. Everyone wanted to see the British band that was making headlines around the world.

"They had the coolest suits, the coolest haircuts, and played the coolest songs on the coolest-looking Rickenbacker guitars, Hofner bass, and Ludwig drumset," he remembers in a blurb on his professional Web site. "And then throw in the screaming teenage girl factor, and you had the coolest band in the world."[5]

Vance, Ellen, and the rest of the world were experiencing the beginning of rock and roll—a musical phenomenon that would eventually change the world. Perhaps that is one reason that DeGeneres loves music and dancing so much today.

DeGeneres says that she does not remember a lot about her childhood. "I try to work on my memory," she said in her book *My Point . . . and I Do Have One*. "I *was* a little girl," she jokes. "I know because my parents say I was."[6]

Because she does not remember a lot from her childhood, DeGeneres looked for photos that her parents might have taken. But, both she and her mother say that the DeGenereses took many more photos of Vance than they did of Ellen.

Apparently, DeGeneres's childhood influenced her more than she likes to imagine. Much later in life, she used some of her observations of childhood as a basis for her humor. In early 2008, on the blog for her television show, she wrote: "The kids today have hardly seen anything new invented at all. When I was a kid, there was always a new, exciting invention like Ziploc bags. Before that, we just had a bag that folded over. The sandwich didn't fall out, but it wasn't fresh. Kids today don't know what stale food tastes like. Today they drink juice from a box. When I was a kid we had to drink right from the orange."[7]

PARENTS' DIVORCE

DeGeneres's great sense of humor as a child and teenager helped her get through many difficult times. Her parents decided to divorce when she was 13 years old. Vance was busy working as a disc jockey and preparing to graduate from high school. Also, he was part of a band that traveled to performances, so Ellen was the one who spent a lot of time with her mother as the divorce was occurring.

She used humor to cheer up her mother, making Betty DeGeneres laugh by imitating her. "My mother was going through some really hard times and I could see when she was really getting down, and I would start to make fun of her dancing," DeGeneres told a reporter for *The New York Times* in 1994. "Then she'd start to laugh, and I'd make fun of her laughing. . . . So I would totally bring her from where I'd seen her start going into depression to all the way out of it. As a 13-year-old kid, I learned I could manipulate people that way. That's a really powerful thing."[8]

After Vance graduated from high school, he began to travel more with his band so Ellen and her mother hung out together a lot. "We were always close," Ellen told an *In Style* writer, "so much so that I used to pretend to be sick to stay home from school."[9]

Just as she was adjusting to her parents' divorce, Ellen's life quickly changed again. When she was a sophomore in high school, her mother remarried and moved to a new home in Atlanta, Texas. Ellen stayed with her father until the school year was over, then she moved to Atlanta to be with her mother and stepfather. Compared with New Orleans, Atlanta was a fairly boring town. It was much smaller and had none of the musical history and interesting restaurants and culture that New Orleans has. Ellen eventually joined the girls' tennis team at the high school, but apparently she was interested in few other activities.

DeGeneres made new friends and started to date. "I was boy-crazy growing up," DeGeneres once told talk-show host Larry King during an interview in 2000. "I was obsessed with boys and men."[10]

During her senior year, she attended the prom with a boy named Richard Reynolds. Many years later, she laughed with *Today* show host Matt Lauer as they looked at a prom picture of her and Reynolds. DeGeneres was wearing a fashionable plaid, halter dress. Soon after, for her own show, DeGeneres flew Reynolds in from his home in Texarkana, Texas, and asked him to put on the suit he wore to the prom so they could re-create the outfits. They thought it was hilarious.

While she was in high school, Ellen also started to become more interested in music. Comedy, it seemed, was not yet part of her career plan. She thought she was in love with a boy who gave her a promise ring, which meant that they would eventually marry. To this day, she makes jokes about his putting her name on the back of his pickup truck in iridescent letters. But Ellen soon found out that marrying him was not what she wanted to do.[11]

HEALING THROUGH LAUGHTER

Around the same time, Ellen had to deal with more stress in her young life. Her mother discovered a lump in her breast that was later diagnosed as cancer. Fairly quickly, Betty DeGeneres had a mastectomy, a surgery that removed part of her breast. Ellen spent hours at the hospital and at home, with her mom as she recuperated from the surgery. Ellen seemed to enjoy entertaining her mother so that she would laugh. "It brought us closer together and made me realize the power of humor," DeGeneres told *Teen People* in a 2006 interview.[12]

DeGeneres, it seems, has always known that laughter is important. In fact, she sometimes makes jokes about laughter on her television show and even wrote about it on her blog. "Laughter is really important," she wrote. "It's probably our greatest invention. I mean, inventing fire was important, but the first laugh probably relieved millions of years of built-up stress."[13]

Ellen went through some very personal turmoil when she was a teen. She was unable to share the problem with her mother until a few years later: Her stepfather had inappropriately touched her breast a few days after her mother's surgery. There were other incidents, too, that proved to Ellen that she could not continue to live with this man. Even though Ellen told a friend about the incidents, the friend's mother told her not to tell Betty DeGeneres while she was still recovering from surgery. This is a decision that DeGeneres still regrets.

"I didn't tell my mother right away because she was going through [her own problems]," she told a writer from *Teen People* in 2006. "So I didn't tell her for a long time. I did tell my best friend's mother, though, and she said, 'Don't tell your mother. It's going to hurt her.' I told other people, and everyone said the same thing. I should have kept going until somebody told my mother. As a kid, I thought adults knew better, but there's really no excuse for someone not telling my mother. I should have been protected."[14]

Even in her comedy today, DeGeneres knows that teens deal with a lot of problems. "The teenage years are the hardest time of life, aren't they?" she asks on her blog. "Teenagers go through so many physical and hormonal changes. . . . Teens think they have all the answers. They think adults are stupid. Guess what? A lot of adults are stupid. As much as you think your parents are stupid, you will become them."[15]

DeGeneres could not wait to escape Atlanta, Texas, after she graduated from high school. The day after she graduated, she moved back to New Orleans with the

Ellen DeGeneres and her mother, Betty, attended the 31st annual Daytime Emmy Awards in 2004 at Radio City Music Hall in New York City. As a teenager, Ellen discovered that her sense of humor helped her mother cope as she was going through a divorce and fighting breast cancer.

help of her father and his new wife. Her plans were to attend the University of New Orleans. But after just a month, DeGeneres dropped out and started to work at various jobs.

Her first job ever was driving cars out of a car wash, and DeGeneres did not mind the task.[16] For a while, she shucked oysters at a restaurant and then moved onto other challenges. She went back to Atlanta a few times, once taking a job checking gloves at the factory where her mother also worked. DeGeneres could not stand that job. "The worst job I ever had, and I lasted a half a day, was I worked in a glove factory in Atlanta, Texas," she told talk-show host Larry King. "It was horrible. . . . I was checking for too many fingers or a hole or something, and gloves would just go by."[17]

DeGeneres turned to comedy as she was figuring out what to do with her life. She told King during an interview that her goal back then was to earn a living. "I was struggling," she said. "I was young and I had nothing going on. I was a waitress and shucked oysters and I sold vacuum cleaners and I painted houses and hated what I was doing. And I hated working, and I needed money."[18]

In the meantime, Vance's popularity on the music scene in New Orleans continued to grow as he became part of the city's New Wave movement. "Everybody knew who he was," DeGeneres remembered during an interview with *People* magazine. "That's what motivated me to do something, because I watched him get all of this attention and glory."[19]

Vance, too, had developed a great sense of humor. Eventually, he and some friends moved to New York City. Their "Mr. Bill" short films became a popular part of the early years of *Saturday Night Live*. By 1977, though, Vance's career faltered, and he decided to join the Marines.

"MOM, I'M GAY"

About a year later, DeGeneres broke some startling news to her mother while visiting her aunt's beach house in Mississippi. "Mom, I'm gay," Betty DeGeneres remembers Ellen telling her as they walked on the beach. DeGeneres was crying. Her startled mother hugged her tight.[20]

Years later, after DeGeneres came out publicly, some people asked her if her stepfather's abuse caused her to become a lesbian. DeGeneres says that there is no relation between the two situations. DeGeneres's mother accepted her daughter's sexuality, writing a book many years later and becoming a mentor to other parents whose children are gay. In the beginning, though, it was trying. Betty DeGeneres thought her daughter was going through a phase.

In the meantime, DeGeneres focused on her comedy. It was with help from Vance's girlfriend, when he returned to New Orleans after two years in the Marines, that DeGeneres finally made her first appearance on stage as part of an annual musical satire put on by the local Gridiron Club.

Soon after that, while still working odd jobs in 1980, DeGeneres started to perform at a coffeehouse at the University of New Orleans. The local newspaper, the *Times Picayune*, even wrote about her. Still, DeGeneres's early career success did not even pay all of her living expenses—like rent, food, and car costs. The old vehicle she drove broke down, and she had to take the bus everywhere. DeGeneres probably thought about giving up on her comedy act. But she didn't.

Eventually she landed a regular gig at a New Orleans club. Unlike other comedians, DeGeneres never liked to use profanity or other obscene humor in her act. She has always been a clean-cut comedian, with sparkling blue eyes and pretty blond hair. Her budding comedy career seemed to be doing very well.

"The more I did it, the more I realized I enjoyed acting out little tiny things on stage," DeGeneres told a writer for the *Chicago Tribune* several years later.[21]

Yet, there was more sadness to come. The young woman with whom DeGeneres was living was killed in an automobile crash. That was a devastating loss. Out of her grief one night, DeGeneres wrote one of the most successful comedy acts of her young career—the conversation with God that she would later recite on Johnny Carson's show.

It seems that the death of her good friend led DeGeneres to make some big decisions. Soon after, she told her mother

IN HER OWN WORDS

Ellen DeGeneres's phone-call-to-God monologue earned her early acclaim. Here is how the routine began, as related in Betty DeGeneres's book, *Love, Ellen*:

> "Hi, God. It's Ellen."
> (a beat, waiting for a response)
> "DeGeneres . . .?"
> (listening to the response)
> "What's so funny?"
> (listening)
> "Oh, yeah, it does sound sort of like that. No, no one's said that before. (a beat) Oh, so, I was just wondering why some things are down here. . . . No, not Charo . . . I'm just wondering why there are fleas here."
> (listening to the response)
> "Oh? No . . . I didn't realize there were so many people employed by the flea collar industry. . . . And flea spray, too. . . . I didn't think about that either."

about the abuse that had occurred. Even though her mother believed her, she could not find the emotional strength to divorce DeGeneres's stepfather for many years after that. "Thinking back, it is my greatest regret that I didn't act immediately and leave once and for all," Betty DeGeneres told Diane Sawyer many years later on ABC's *Good Morning America*. "I am so blessed that our relationship not only survived it, we're closer and stronger."[22]

Within months, DeGeneres made another very risky decision. She planned to move to San Francisco by herself. The comedy scene there was thriving, with many young people trying to make their way in the profession. Even though it was a challenging choice to move to California alone, DeGeneres seemed to know what lay in her future— she was out to become a star.

The Funniest
Person in America

Even though San Francisco was a lot of fun, DeGeneres missed her family and friends. San Francisco was a beautiful city, but it was also expensive to live there. And, trying to become a famous comedian was not easy, by far. The competition among local comedians—most of them men—was fierce.

DeGeneres was not there long before she decided to move back to New Orleans, where she took a daytime job in a law firm and appeared at comedy clubs in the evening. She would have much preferred just working on her comedy, but she needed money to pay her expenses. "Everything I did that was a 9-to-5 job I hated," DeGeneres said in an interview much later in life. "Being in an office . . . I just hated being in an office."[1]

For a short while, DeGeneres's mother moved in with her and contemplated divorcing her husband. Betty DeGeneres, however, decided to return to Atlanta, Texas, so she could finish college and earn a living on her own. DeGeneres tried to understand her mother's predicament—a smart woman whom she loved a lot stuck in a marriage to a man DeGeneres did not trust much.

Nonetheless, DeGeneres continued to work hard to achieve her own dreams. One day, even though she had a fever, she competed at a local club for the title of the Funniest Person in New Orleans. Several other comedians were vying for the award, with a panel of judges determining who was the funniest. She won the local contest.

A tape of her performance from that evening was entered into a contest that the Showtime network was sponsoring called the Funniest Person in Louisiana. Again, several days later, DeGeneres was pronounced the winner. The tape was forwarded to judges in New York City to compete for Showtime's Funniest Person in America contest.

In the meantime, DeGeneres decided to move back to San Francisco. As she was saving for the trip, she and her brother decided to do a farewell show at the Toulouse Theater in New Orleans to help her raise money for the move. Vance served as the master of ceremonies, while DeGeneres performed her comedy. They threw a going-away party for DeGeneres after the show. It had been only two years since she had returned to New Orleans, but she left her hometown again. She was 26 years old, and she was determined to make it on her own.

BACK TO SAN FRANCISCO

She received some big news soon after she arrived in San Francisco. Although DeGeneres had gotten a few hints earlier that she might be the person chosen for the

Showtime award, she eagerly waited for the final decision to be announced. Shortly after she was settled in her new home, DeGeneres received the news: She had been selected by a panel of well-known comedians to be Showtime's first-ever Funniest Person in America.

Along with the exciting title, DeGeneres was invited to appear on Showtime. The network taped one of her performances in a New York City nightclub and created three short segments from it—one was about 10 minutes long and the other two were five minutes long. Showtime plugged those segments into its programming and made DeGeneres part of the *Comic of the Month* series.[2]

In addition, DeGeneres got an agent who helped her book shows. She started to travel around the country to perform in small clubs in tiny towns as well as in well-known comedy clubs in bigger cities. Besides performing, DeGeneres's responsibilities included looking for the comedian who would be named the next Funniest Person in America.

Her new title worked well for DeGeneres. Clubs more readily opened their doors to her, but all was not perfect with the Funniest Person in America. DeGeneres experienced jealousy and bitterness from some comedians—and audiences—that she met along the way. She remembers one performance at a club in San Francisco, when the front row of the audience—mostly men—turned their backs on her while she was onstage. "I was crying," she told a *New York Times* writer years later. "I wanted to go home and get out of the business. I thought, 'This is the worst business; it's so cruel.' "[3]

Nonetheless, DeGeneres stayed focused on her goal in life. As she toured comedy clubs around the country, she tried to live off of the income from her performances and her Showtime title. Even as the Funniest Person in America, DeGeneres lived on a very tight budget.

In this photograph from the 1980s, Ellen DeGeneres is performing her stand-up act at a comedy club. In 1982, DeGeneres was named Showtime's Funniest Person in America. As a result, she began to book more appearances at clubs around the country.

"I definitely came from a lower-middle-class family," DeGeneres once told a newspaper reporter. "I never really had money. I never had connections in the business. Every little, tiny move up the mountain hasn't been a big deal to me. . . . I've come a long way. But since I've been with myself every step of the way, I didn't really notice such a huge stride."[4]

By any standard, though, DeGeneres's stint as the Funniest Person in America was a success. Often, she got to be the first comedian onstage during several of the tryouts for the next Funniest Person in America. On August 27,

1984, DeGeneres did a brief stand-up show before a lunch-time crowd on the plaza of the former World Trade Center in New York City. After that, nearly 60 other comedians competed for DeGeneres's title as several judges watched their acts.[5] This was the first stop for Showtime's mobile television production van as it cruised the country and visited 21 cities, filming dozens of comedians along the way. In addition, the network solicited videotapes from other comedians across the country. The search was on for DeGeneres's replacement.

A few days after the New York show, at a club in Boston, 35 comedians competed for the title. The competition was close as about 100 people sat in the audience and watched.[6] Perhaps DeGeneres's surge in popularity during the year that she traveled the country created even more interest among comedians who now desperately wanted the title.

After 45 statewide winners were named, Showtime finally selected its second Funniest Person in America in June 1985. The winner was Phil Nee of New York. During the competition, DeGeneres had even more great experiences. She had the chance to work with some well-known comedians of the time, including David Brenner, Gabe Kaplan, and Carl Reiner. All three had helped judge the Funniest Person in America contest.

Not long after that, DeGeneres was a guest comedian at a Beverly Hills fund-raiser for the Advertising Industry Emergency Fund. The event was at the glitzy Beverly Hilton Hotel in Los Angeles, and DeGeneres appeared with two other comedians—Bill Maher and Sinbad, who only went by one name. The three of them helped to raise $50,000 for the emergency fund.[7] It seemed that, after her year with Showtime, DeGeneres had become one of the most sought-after comedians in the country.

HEADED TO L.A.

Soon, she began to dream about moving to Los Angeles. She felt that living there would be good for her career. DeGeneres was hoping to appear in television and films, and she knew she should be in Los Angeles to pursue that dream. When she moved to the city, though, she found that living there was difficult. It was similar to her first move to San Francisco: Competition was terribly challenging, and everything was expensive. DeGeneres started to get depressed over the situation when a big break came her way.

The comedian Johnny Carson invited her to appear on his late-night talk show. Most comedians who appeared on *The Tonight Show* did their routines and then went off stage. DeGeneres got a rare invitation—to join Carson on the couch for a chat. Perhaps this was a sign of what was to come much later in life for DeGeneres—when she experienced other groundbreaking opportunities for women in comedy, such as hosting the Emmys and the Oscars.

Soon after appearing on Carson's show, DeGeneres was part of Home Box Office's tenth annual special called *The Young Comedians All-Star Reunion.* "Many of the aspirants are never heard from again," John J. O'Connor wrote in *The New York Times.*[8] In fact, DeGeneres was one of those aspiring young comedians who did make it to the top—as were Jay Leno, who was on the HBO special in 1976, and comedian Paul Reubens, who called himself Pee-wee Herman and had been on the show in 1980.

DeGeneres's career was taking off. Carson invited her back to his show several times over the next few months, and national magazines began to write about her success. Finally, DeGeneres started to earn thousands of dollars for each of her appearances. When HBO filmed its *One-Night Stand* comedy special in 1989 at the Fillmore in

San Francisco, DeGeneres was considered a hometown comedian. She headlined the show with other comedians, including Will Durst and Jake Johannsen.[9]

HER FIRST SITCOM

By now, DeGeneres's life had taken a dramatic turn. It was a very exciting time, compared with those slow days she spent as a teenager in Atlanta, Texas. In 1989, DeGeneres won a part in a Fox television sitcom called *Open House*. On the show, she played Margo Van Meter, a zany receptionist at a real estate office. Even though the show lasted only one season, DeGeneres's portrayal of Margo made some Hollywood executives take notice of this young star.[10]

DeGeneres appreciated the experience of working on her first television show, despite its short tenure. "*Open House* was a wonderful springboard. . . . It was a good place for me to grow for a year," she said.[11]

Twice, in the late 1980s, DeGeneres was nominated for an American Comedy Award. She continued to play clubs around the country and draw crowds that appreciated her comedy. In 1991, she was finally named the Best Female Stand-Up at the American Comedy Awards.[12]

In the meantime, DeGeneres's mother finally left her husband and moved to Los Angeles, where Ellen and Vance were living. Betty DeGeneres had earned her college degree, and she went to work as a speech therapist. Ellen was happy to have her mother closer and looked forward to seeing her more often.

Ellen DeGeneres's future as a comedian looked bright. The number of female comedians was increasing. In 1992, DeGeneres was one of 24 female comics who were featured in a documentary film called *Wisecracks*, which was about society's feelings regarding female stand-ups. "My grandmother, she started walking five miles a day when she was

Ellen DeGeneres is seen in a publicity shot for the 1989–1990 Fox sitcom *Open House*. The show, which lasted only one season, was DeGeneres's first TV series. She played wacky receptionist Margo Van Meter.

60," DeGeneres quipped on the film. "She's 97 today, and we don't know where the (heck) she is."[13]

In the 1980s, comedy was still a career that most women didn't consider, even though there were several women older than DeGeneres who were famous for making people laugh: Lucille Ball, Phyllis Diller, and Joan Rivers

LUCILLE BALL

As she was growing up, one of Ellen DeGeneres's favorite female comedians was Lucille Ball, who starred in various half-hour sitcoms for more than 20 years. DeGeneres's humor was nourished by watching reruns of Ball's hilarious first show, *I Love Lucy*, as well as the different incarnations of her sitcoms that followed. Ball was one of the first women recognized as being funny. Her observational style of humor reminded DeGeneres of her own comedic impulses.

Ball was born on August 6, 1911, in Jamestown, New York, to Henry D. and Desiree Hunt Ball. She attended the Chautauqua Institute of Music and the John Murray Anderson-Robert Milton Dramatic School in New York City. Ball began to appear in films in the mid-1930s.

In 1940, she married Desi Arnaz, a Cuban musician who later played a band conductor named Ricky Ricardo on *I Love Lucy*, which aired from 1951 to 1957. In 1952, *I Love Lucy* made TV history when Ball's second pregnancy was written into the show. Never before had an actress's pregnancy been part of a television series. A priest, a minister, and a rabbi previewed each show before it aired to be sure it wasn't offensive. The couple had two children: Lucie Desiree Arnaz was born in 1951, and Desi Arnaz Jr., was born in 1953.

were among them. Also interviewed for the documentary were popular comedians of that time, including Paula Poundstone, Whoopi Goldberg, and Jenny Jones.[14]

"I can't believe that anyone would still have a problem with women being funny," DeGeneres told a reporter after the documentary was made. "What century is that? I guess

Although *I Love Lucy* finished filming in 1957, stations around the United States ran plenty of the show's reruns for decades. Ball and Arnaz did *The Lucy-Desi Comedy Hour* on CBS from 1957 to 1960. In 1960, though, the couple's marriage ended and so did the show. Ball married Gary Morton, a stand-up comedian, in 1961.

From 1962 to 1968, Ball continued her success with *The Lucy Show* on CBS. Another program followed called *Here's Lucy*, which ran on CBS from 1968 to 1974. In 1986, ABC briefly aired a show called *Life with Lucy*. Three years later, Ball died at Cedars Sinai Medical Center in Los Angeles after suffering a heart attack. She was 77.

Ball's achievements in humor were recognized after her death when she was awarded the TV Land Legacy of Laughter Award at the Emmy Awards in 2007. Throughout her career, Ball won multiple Emmy Awards, including Best Comedienne in 1952 and Best Actress in a Continuing Performance in 1955.

I Love Lucy, her initial sitcom, continues to be seen in 77 countries and is dubbed in 22 languages. It is said that Ball led the way for the female comedians who would emerge in later years, including Phyllis Diller, Joan Rivers, Carol Burnett, Lily Tomlin, and others.

they're the same people who think that a football player can't do needlepoint or take ballet."[15]

Still, DeGeneres's humor came across loud and clear. She began to look at comedy as an art, like painting or writing. It was a creative outlet that gave her the satisfaction of knowing that others appreciated her work. "I don't think my fans enjoy being spoon-fed," DeGeneres once told a reporter. "I paint pictures with words, and you put it together in your mind. People like to do a little work."[16]

DeGeneres appeared on another HBO *One Night Stand*—this one was filmed at the Paragon in Miami Beach, Florida. She did a commercial for the AT&T phone company in which she played a pet shop owner—a natural role considering DeGeneres's love of animals. In 1993, she had a memorable performance at the University of California in Los Angeles. It was like déjà vu: Vance was the master of ceremonies just as he had been at his sister's going-away performance in New Orleans.

Ellen DeGeneres was working very hard, as if she hoped that every new experience would add up to stardom. She enjoyed her work and continued to improve her comedy. She loved to make people laugh. After she appeared on *One Night Stand*, she told a *Chicago Tribune* reporter that it was a great boost to her career. "It has been terrific, because it definitely elevates you to the next level," she said.[17]

In the early 1990s, DeGeneres had an opportunity for her career to expand. She landed her second television series, winning the role of a nurse on *Laurie Hill*, a short-lived sitcom that aired on ABC in 1992. Even though *Laurie Hill* did not last long, it turned out to be a stepping-stone to more television success.

A Television Star

Despite the failure of *Laurie Hill*, Ellen DeGeneres's career as a comedian continued to be busy. In a small city in New York, during an evening show in June 1994, DeGeneres joked about the mating habits of various animals. Penguins are monogamous because they all look alike, she quipped. There's no need to leave your mate for a better-looking prospect.[1]

DeGeneres continued to polish her stand-up comedy act. She knew that show business was not easy, but she was willing to continue working hard toward her goal. Certainly, DeGeneres was persistent.

Soon after the cancellation of *Laurie Hill*, ABC approached DeGeneres about a television show in which she would have a significant role. DeGeneres was thrilled.

The show was to be called *These Friends of Mine*, and it focused on a woman named Ellen Morgan, who would be played by DeGeneres, and her friendships with two single women and a man.

From the time DeGeneres read the first script, she thought the show could be very funny. "I was laughing out loud when I read the script," DeGeneres recalled later. "I knew what I could do with it. I wanted to do a smarter, hipper version of *I Love Lucy*. . . . I wanted a show that everybody talks about the next day."[2]

As the show evolved, Ellen Morgan worked in a bookstore and coffeehouse based in Los Angeles, where she hung out with her best friends. Ellen Morgan was a bit klutzy and awkward. Even though DeGeneres did not write the scripts for the show, she ad-libbed funny lines during each episode.

Once filming was under way for *These Friends of Mine*, there was a brief interruption when DeGeneres was hospitalized with a ruptured ovarian cyst.[3] Within days, though, she was back at work. When it was finally time to air the new sitcom, *These Friends of Mine* appeared on ABC right after another popular show, *Home Improvement*, which featured comedian Tim Allen. Within the first four weeks of its debut in March 1994, *These Friends of Mine* was a hit—ranked among the top 10 television shows.[4]

DeGeneres said that, unlike her Margo character on the earlier television show *Open House*, Ellen Morgan was

DID YOU KNOW?

Ellen DeGeneres was originally offered Sandra Bullock's role in the 1994 action film *Speed*, but she turned it down. DeGeneres also turned down an offer to be one of the regulars on the TV series *Friends*.

a character that was just like herself. In the show's first episode, Ellen Morgan obsessed over her driver's license photo. "I try to do stuff that makes people think about their own experiences," DeGeneres explained to a reporter for the *Detroit Free Press*.[5] DeGeneres was visiting Detroit for a stand-up appearance, which she continued to do while shooting the first season of *These Friends of Mine*.

DeGeneres was continuously compared with comedian Jerry Seinfeld, who had his own sitcom. It was a time in television when many comedians starred in their own shows: Roseanne Barr, Tim Allen, and Brett Butler. DeGeneres became part of this popular television trend. It seemed as if television producers knew that many of the good stand-up comedians could have hit sitcoms if they had the chance.

Certainly, DeGeneres had come a long way from her first performance, when she stood onstage and ate a Whopper, fries, and a shake in order to entertain the crowd.[6] It had been nearly a dozen years since she had left New Orleans, and DeGeneres still had a slight Southern accent as she did interviews with magazine writers and newspaper reporters. She hinted that her stand-up career might be coming to an end as she wanted to focus more on television and movies. Yet, DeGeneres's stand-up fans still loved her. While appearing at a theater in northern Indiana one evening, she received rave reviews. Fans rushed to the stage to give her roses and notes. "DeGeneres is an animated storyteller, working jokes in while reacting to her audience," a critic for the *Chicago Tribune* wrote after the show. Once again DeGeneres was compared with Jerry Seinfeld. "The cooler Seinfeld does a lot of one-liners and tends to stay a little detached," the critic wrote.[7]

ABC wanted to make sure that DeGeneres's new show was a success, so she agreed to meet with the media. One day, she showed up at a restaurant called B. Smith's to meet a reporter from *The New York Times*. DeGeneres was her usual, casual self. She wore jeans, a white T-shirt, a pin-striped blazer, and no makeup. She also had on a little hat, backward. The reporter talked to her about the comparisons to Seinfeld. "I love Jerry," DeGeneres told the reporter. "I think he's got a great show. But I've always been compared to Jerry. And, if you saw my act, we're not very much alike at all."[8]

JERRY SEINFELD

When *These Friends of Mine* began to air in 1994, a lot of people thought that the show was just a different version of *Seinfeld*, a successful television program whose main character, Jerry Seinfeld, was a stand-up comedian. *Seinfeld* featured three main male characters and one female character—opposite of the cast of *These Friends of Mine*.

But Ellen DeGeneres, and a lot of television critics, disagreed that the two series were mirrors of each other. They said that DeGeneres's humor was different from Seinfeld's, that her humor was not as blunt as his. Nonetheless, it certainly was not bad for DeGeneres's show to be compared with one created by Seinfeld, who is one of the most popular male stand-up comedians.

Even today, Seinfeld is the top-earning comedian alive, and he hasn't done his television show for 10 years. *Forbes* estimates his annual income to be $60 million, mainly based on money he still earns from reruns of the 175 *Seinfeld* episodes.*

Seinfeld was born on April 29, 1954, in Brooklyn, New York, and his parents later moved the family to Long Island. He has one sister, Carolyn, and his father was a commercial sign maker with a good sense of humor. Seinfeld first attended the State

Being likened to Seinfeld at the time wasn't a bad thing for DeGeneres, though. Seinfeld was also a stand-up comedian who worked very hard to achieve success. He attended Queens College and started his comedy career in Manhattan clubs, eventually starring in a sitcom called *Seinfeld*. The show, which ran from 1989 to 1998 on NBC, was one of television's most popular sitcoms.

University of New York at Oswego in upstate New York but then returned to the city to continue his studies at Queens College. He started to do stand-up while in college and later tried out on amateur night at New York's Catch a Rising Star in 1976.**

Similar to what would happen to DeGeneres a few years later, Seinfeld's career took off after appearing on *The Tonight Show* starring Johnny Carson in 1981. In 1989, he and stand-up buddy Larry David were invited to create a sitcom for NBC. The popular *Seinfeld* episodes aired from 1989 to 1998.

Even after his television show ended, Seinfeld continued to be extremely popular. He infrequently makes public appearances but has released several books and television specials, including *The Seinfeld Story*, a 2004 documentary. In 2007, Seinfeld appeared in *Bee Movie*.

He has been married to Jessica Seinfeld since December 1999, and they have three children.

---

*Lacey Rose, "The Top-Earning Comedians," *Forbes*. October 11, 2007.
**"Biography for Jerry Seinfeld." Internet Movie Database. Available online at http://www.imdb.com.

Jerry Seinfeld *(right)* appears in an episode of his hit sitcom, *Seinfeld*, along with Jason Alexander and Julia Louis-Dreyfus. As a comedian, Seinfeld was also known for his observational humor. Critics often compared Ellen DeGeneres's style, and her new series, *These Friends of Mine*, to Seinfeld and his show.

'DRESS'ED FOR SUCCESS

DeGeneres was quickly becoming in demand. In September 1994, she hosted the Emmy Awards for the first time in her career. She loved the experience but said later that the biggest problem was having to wear a dress. "I hate dresses," she said, adding that she had not worn one since 1980.[9] "I thought I looked . . . I don't know . . . big. I'm too muscular to wear a dress." Before the show, DeGeneres started to kick-box and lost some weight so that she would look better in the dress.

In the end, she did wear a dress during the evening of the Emmys at the Pasadena Civic Auditorium. It was an elegant black dress adorned with rhinestones that was designed by Donna Karan. And DeGeneres was a hit—both for her fashionable attire and for the humor she sprinkled throughout the show. A week later, she met with a reporter from *USA Today* and, as they sipped drinks at a West Hollywood coffee shop, she talked about all the attention she was receiving after hosting the show.

Movie companies were calling, too, yet DeGeneres was careful about the projects she considered. She wanted to be sure that she had some control over how she was portrayed in a film. "It feels like this is all really what's supposed to be happening," she said in the middle of 1994. "It doesn't seem like it's all there yet. I think I have a lot further to go, and I think I can achieve a lot more."[10]

Soon after *These Friends of Mine* was launched, DeGeneres was signed to star in the Disney film *Mr. Wrong*. The filming for the movie was scheduled to take place during the break for her television show.

In the film, DeGeneres starred as Martha, a 31-year-old woman who had never had a serious relationship. Finally, she meets a wealthy investor and falls in love—he's ruggedly handsome and sensitive and seems nearly too good to be true. It turns out that the man is obsessively psychotic and won't let go of the relationship. Film critics said that *Mr. Wrong* was a silly movie. Unfortunately, the movie did not seem to boost DeGeneres's career much. Yet, she did get some accolades for her appearance in it. "She's blessed with a congenial, likable personality that gets you smiling just by looking at her," a movie critic from *The Miami Herald* reported, "and that quality has survived the big-screen leap."[11]

During DeGeneres's first season on her hit television show, she was nominated for an Emmy award as best actress. When she attended the awards ceremony in September 1995—a year after she had hosted them—both she and comedian Rosie O'Donnell wore diamonds that were on loan from jeweler Harry Winston. "Look at yours!" *People* magazine reported that DeGeneres yelled when she saw O'Donnell. "I thought mine was big!"[12] It was rare that DeGeneres dressed up for these Hollywood occasions.

For example, the following year, she attended a fundraiser at the home of actress Goldie Hawn in Pacific Palisades, a community just outside of Hollywood. DeGeneres wore a plaid shirt and white pants when nearly everyone else wore fancier clothes.[13] Still, being dressed more casually than everyone else did not seem to bother her a bit. DeGeneres always wanted to be comfortable in whatever she chose to wear. She knew that how she dressed really did not say anything about the kind of person she was. DeGeneres has always enjoyed making jokes about her choice of clothing, even saying that she had shown up at parties twice in the exact same outfit as someone else—that someone else, she said, was older actor William Shatner.[14]

Other comedians at that time had written books at the height of their popularity, and DeGeneres followed suit as she was also offered a book contract. Even in her book, she discussed how she did not like to wear dresses and how people should not be judged by the way they dress. To this

Ellen DeGeneres played opposite Bill Pullman in her first feature film, *Mr. Wrong*, which was about a woman who fell in love with a psychotic man. Most of the reviews for the film were poor, although a few found some charm in DeGeneres's performance.

day, DeGeneres tries always to look her best, but no one would call her a fashion icon.

During this period in DeGeneres's life, she seemed to become very popular on the social circuit. Suddenly, she was on the A-list for invitations. She was among a select group of celebrities invited to the grand opening of the first Hard Rock Hotel, which was in Las Vegas. DeGeneres received an invitation, complete with poker chips featuring the image of rock-and-roll legend Jimi Hendrix. Also attending the party were Kevin Costner, Kelsey Grammer, supermodel Christy Turlington, and others.[15]

DeGeneres found that being a television star was quickly changing her life. "You get a TV show, and you suddenly become this person who is watched and studied," she said.[16] There were a lot of good aspects to being famous—such as the parties and the popularity—but DeGeneres would eventually find out that there was a negative side, too.

ADD AUTHOR TO THE LIST

By the mid-1990s, DeGeneres was more popular than she had ever been in her professional life. A calendar was even produced with her face on it! She wrote her first book, *My Point . . . And I Do Have One*, although apparently she had some trouble trying to come up with the 60,000 words that the publisher sought. The last chapter focused on how hard it was to write a 60,000-word book.

DeGeneres focused on funny stories and jokes, with chapter titles such as "A Frog in a Sombrero Does Not a Party Make" and "The Ellie-Gellie." Some critics thought that the book should be more serious, even though it sold a lot of copies. "I have no doubt that there is a really good book in Ellen DeGeneres," a critic from *The Buffalo News*

IN HER OWN WORDS

Ellen DeGeneres's 1995 book, *My Point . . . And I Do Have One*, became a best seller. In "A Note from the Author," DeGeneres offered readers a little insight into what was to come:

> As you may have noticed, my mind does not work the same as most. That is to say, I'm sort of, well—different— and yet it seems to have worked for me.

wrote. "One that describes what it's like to go through the growing pains of a hit show. One that frankly discusses her personal life."[17]

But DeGeneres did not want to write that kind of book. In fact, in all of the interviews she did with the media during her years of growing success, she kept quiet about her personal life. DeGeneres would frequently say that she was happy, but she did not respond to personal questions. She would talk about other topics, such as the two dogs she had at home, but when questions came up about her love life, she became a pro at avoiding them.

In her book, DeGeneres stuck to silly jokes and wry humor. Even though her family was well aware that she was gay, she was not ready to discuss that aspect of her personal life openly. In fact, it would be a few more years before DeGeneres would even mention her sexuality in public.

Nonetheless, most of her close friends and family knew about her sexuality. Privately, DeGeneres shared that she was gay with people who she thought should know. When she met with a leading agent for comedians after moving to San Francisco in 1984, she mentioned it to him because she thought her sexuality might affect her career. "I want you to know something," she told the agent. "I'm gay." The agent was unfazed. "She was very relieved it wasn't an issue," he recalled.[18]

After the first season, *These Friends of Mine* was renamed *Ellen*, with DeGeneres in the lead role. The show's executive producer said the shift from an ensemble cast of several important characters to DeGeneres being the star of the show was a good change. Also, some of the cast was replaced, and the show's two original creators and writers left. Newspaper and magazine reporters started to write about the big shakeup. DeGeneres took it in stride, saying that changes were made without her being involved. She did point out a few times, however, that she refused to do some of the original episodes the year before because they contained language that she did not want to use. "I truly am an innocent bystander," she told a reporter for The Associated Press. "I don't know what people may think, that I'm like this tyrant really. But I was just praying that we got picked up again."[19]

Just before the second season opened, DeGeneres decided that she would no longer tour as a stand-up comic. "I'm not doing it anymore," she said. "I think I've retired."[20]

Nonetheless, DeGeneres knew that, after years and years of hard work, she was finally getting a big chance at stardom. In the second season of the show, Ellen Morgan had a different hairstyle, and she became the owner of the bookstore, which was called "Buy the Book."[21]

DeGeneres tried not to let her success go to her head. "You can't help but start thinking, 'I'm really special,'" she once told a reporter. "And you have to really, really be prepared and know you are not special."[22] DeGeneres continued to make jokes about everything. She saw the humor in the new, expensive hair salon she went to and the smock boys and shampoo boys who worked there. Still, she stayed grounded, once telling a reporter that cleaning up after her dog was a reminder that she really was not that important.

In the meantime, DeGeneres was focused on her show, looking for ways to improve it. People talked about her success on television, but DeGeneres knew that there was room to get better. "If I'm the queen of show business—that'll take another year or so," she once joked with a newspaper reporter. "I think the characters, all the characters, need a lot more development."[23]

Despite her enthusiasm and excitement about the new *Ellen* show, becoming a famous television star was not always fun. "This whole celebrity thing is such a strange thing to handle," she said. "You're not trained for how people react to you, because you're so busy working."[24]

After the first season, the name of *These Friends of Mine* was changed to *Ellen*, with the show focused more on Ellen DeGeneres's character. Here, she appears in a publicity shot for *Ellen* along with David Anthony Higgins *(standing)*, Joely Fisher *(seated, left)*, and Arye Gross.

Certainly, DeGeneres was not used to being recognized on the street when she went out to do casual errands.

Continually, there was gossip in the tabloids that DeGeneres treated the people on the show's staff poorly and that many were leaving because of that. And, on occasion, DeGeneres admitted that she missed doing her stand-up act. "I miss being onstage and getting into that rhythm where there's this amazing high," she said during a news conference.[25]

Despite its original success, *Ellen* started to lose some of its popularity by the middle of its second season. The rumors that DeGeneres was difficult to work with continued, but she defended herself, saying such comments were not true. "Sometimes, I don't exert this power that everybody believes I have," DeGeneres said during a press conference to promote *Mr. Wrong*. "Sometimes I really just want to have a life. I don't want it to be a 24-hour-a-day job."[26]

DeGeneres had stopped doing stand-up, and she stopped watching other comedians, too. She simply did not have enough time. While doing her sitcom, DeGeneres received an interesting proposal. She was approached a few times by companies that wanted her to do a talk show. It was as if there was a sign that she should move in that direction. Rosie O'Donnell, another popular comedian, had just started her own talk show. DeGeneres, though, did not want to appear to be a copycat. She refused to consider the idea, saying that perhaps she would do a talk show later in life.

Meanwhile, her sitcom drew accolades. She won a People's Choice Award in 1995, had two Golden Globe nominations, two Screen Actors Guild Award nominations, and an Emmy nomination.

Despite the awards, *Ellen* still struggled for an identity. DeGeneres certainly brought a lot of humor to the show, but the writers had a difficult time developing the characters, including DeGeneres's. In addition, the time and day that the program was shown moved several times. "We're still trying to find out exactly what the show is," DeGeneres said at the time. "And I think what's hurt us so much is that we've moved like 25 times since we've been on the air." [27]

One exciting episode was taped on DeGeneres's thirty-eighth birthday. Mary Tyler Moore was the guest star, and she tried to assist DeGeneres during the show, when the star was trying to save a lobster from being eaten. (DeGeneres's character was a vegetarian.)

Other celebrities made guest appearances, too. During one episode, Martha Stewart was an unexpected guest at a dinner party hosted by Ellen Morgan. A cooking disaster occurred and, in the end, Ellen Morgan ended up throwing Cornish hens at her guests.

As DeGeneres struggled to find the perfect niche for her show, her career heated up in other ways. She was invited to host the thirty-eighth annual Grammy Awards at the Shrine Auditorium in Los Angeles. "Her talent, edge, and wit will be a tremendous plus for the telecast," said Michael Greene, the president of the National Academy of Recording Arts and Sciences, which presents the Grammys.[28] While the awards show was airing live on one channel on February 28, 1996, *Ellen* was being shown on another network. Two shows starring Ellen DeGeneres were competing with each other. Several months later, in September, DeGeneres again hosted the Emmy Awards.

Still, the ratings for *Ellen* continued to slump a bit. And, DeGeneres ran into ongoing criticism. One *Time* magazine article said that she had failed to integrate her stand-up talents within the confines of the sitcom. And as the show continued into the following year, more and more questions arose about why DeGeneres's character did not have a serious relationship with a man.[29]

Life Changes

It was the fall of 1996 when the rumors began. Just after the fourth season of her sitcom started, Ellen DeGeneres publicly mentioned having a secret. She began to drop hints: Ellen Morgan might reveal that she is a lesbian during an episode of the show. These suggestions were subtle, yet the media started to buzz and people began to talk. Everyone wondered what was going to happen with *Ellen*.

The first episode of DeGeneres's fourth season was disappointing. The show ranked fifty-second for the week, and ratings had dropped 28 percent from the opener of the previous season.[1] Perhaps those involved with the show, including DeGeneres herself, thought that the banter about Ellen's secret being revealed would improve ratings.

TESTING THE WATERS

In the meantime, DeGeneres released a comedy CD, called *Taste This*. She visited the talk shows of David Letterman, Rosie O'Donnell, and Conan O'Brien. During her appearances, it seemed, she was trying to determine if the world was ready for Ellen Morgan to come out regarding her sexuality. On Letterman, in fact, the audience cheered at the idea of a public coming out.[2] DeGeneres was, perhaps, trying to see if it would be acceptable for her television character to be gay.

At the same time, some people started to notice innuendo in the scripts of *Ellen*. In one episode, Ellen Morgan burst out from behind a door and yelled, "I was in the closet!"[3]

Whether Ellen Morgan would be outed during the weekly sitcom became a guessing game for anyone familiar with the show. A Web site was even created for fans as they watched for signals regarding what was to come that season. DeGeneres admitted during an event at the Museum of Television and Radio in Los Angeles that it was a risk to the show's popularity for Ellen Morgan to come out as a lesbian. "Whatever happens, it would be a risk," she said. "And, yes, it is a risk that I would be willing to take."[4]

But, for Ellen DeGeneres, having Ellen Morgan come out during the television show was not an easy decision. For one, she was concerned that there would be a backlash from the companies that advertised on the show. Yet, the idea of Ellen Morgan announcing that she was a lesbian became important to gay people around the world. To date, no other leading character on a television show was gay, even though at least 20 other gay supporting characters appeared on popular television shows at that time.[5]

Throughout the season, from the fall of 1996 to early 1997, media critics and *Ellen*'s viewers continued to debate the issue. In the meantime, the show's star was also thinking about publicly coming out. DeGeneres's publicists offered interviews with her to several television programs. During these interviews, they promised, DeGeneres would talk about being gay—unlike in the past, when she had kept quiet about her personal life.

As 1997 dawned, Ellen Morgan still had made no announcement on the sitcom, nor had Ellen DeGeneres made a public announcement. Behind the scenes, network executives for ABC and Disney (which was an owner of ABC) were discussing the issue. The executives wanted final approval for the coming-out script once it was written.[6]

Finally, a script was prepared. The show's writers jokingly referred to the episode as "The Puppy Episode." The name was really an inside joke. When *Ellen*'s writers were struggling for storylines, they considered at one point having Ellen get a puppy. Instead, "The Puppy Episode" really referred to the episode regarding Ellen Morgan's coming out. DeGeneres, it seems, had convinced the show's producers that it would be fine for Ellen Morgan to come out. She seemed sure that there would be plenty of storylines to follow after that.

OUT OF THE CLOSET

In the meantime, DeGeneres decided that she would, indeed, talk about being gay. She came out publicly in a cover story in *Time* magazine's April 14, 1997, issue. It was just a couple of weeks before the *Ellen* show had its own coming out. "I hate that term 'in the closet,'" DeGeneres told the *Time* writer. "Until recently I hated the word lesbian, too . . . so I used the word gay more often."[7]

DeGeneres talked about why she had kept her homosexuality quiet until that point. She discussed why she never wanted her private life mixed up with her public life. She said that she always wanted to keep the two separate but

As viewers were wondering if Ellen DeGeneres's character would come out on the sitcom, DeGeneres decided that she would talk about her sexuality publicly. Her interview with *Time* magazine, disclosing that she is a lesbian, was the cover story of the April 14, 1997 issue.

the time had come to, perhaps, be more open. "I mean, I really tried to figure out every way to avoid answering that question for as long as I could," she said. "For me this has been the most freeing experience because people can't hurt me anymore. I don't have to worry about somebody saying something about me, or a reporter trying to find out information."[8]

Meanwhile, viewers anticipated the coming-out show. Behind the scenes, more work was taking place. The original script was rejected by one of the producers, who said it focused too much on the reaction of Ellen Morgan's friends as opposed to Ellen's true feelings. The writers, with DeGeneres's help, kept writing. Oprah Winfrey agreed to make a guest appearance on the show, as a therapist who talked to Ellen Morgan. Actresses Laura Dern and Demi Moore and actor and director Billy Bob Thornton also agreed to guest appearances, as did DeGeneres's gay friends Melissa Etheridge and k.d. lang.

Not everyone was supportive of DeGeneres's revelation, though. Televangelist Jerry Falwell began referring to her as "Ellen Degenerate." In turn, DeGeneres made a joke about Falwell's comment. "Really, he called me that?" she said to

IN HER OWN WORDS

In her interview with *Time* magazine, Ellen DeGeneres spoke about the freedom she felt after she decided to reveal her sexuality publicly. She said:

Literally, as soon as I made this decision, I lost weight. My skin has cleared up. I don't have anything to be scared of, which I think outweighs whatever else happens in my career.

a *Time* magazine reporter. "I've been getting that since the fourth grade. I guess I'm happy I could give him work."[9]

There were other disappointments, too. Two of the show's occasional sponsors, Chrysler and JCPenney, pulled advertising from the program.[10] At least one local television station refused to air the coming-out episode. Just as the episode was being filmed, a soundstage at the Disney studio in Burbank had to be cleared and bomb-sniffing dogs were brought in—because of a telephone threat that was received.[11] Apparently, not everyone was excited about this phase of *Ellen*.

Nonetheless, gay advocates across the country were hopeful. Even though ABC refused to accept an advertisement from the Human Rights Campaign, an organization that offers support to homosexuals, 31 ABC affiliates around the country decided to run the ad.[12]

Finally, on April 30, 1997, the show was scheduled to air in a special one-hour episode. Gay organizations planned "Come Out With Ellen" parties across the country. "I hope it does what Ellen intends, and that's to send a positive message about lesbians and gays in general to the American public," said Vance DeGeneres, who was a writer for the show at the time. Always the big brother, Vance fretted that Ellen could be physically harmed or that she could be typecast once the episode aired.[13] Unfortunately, coming out as a gay person was not always acceptable to everyone. Some people just did not seem to understand.

ABC and Disney officials seemed pleased with the results of the final script. "We think Ellen and the show's staff have executed it beautifully," Jamie Tarses, the president of ABC Entertainment, told a *Time* magazine reporter. "Obviously this is an experiment. We're not sociologists. We don't know how this is going to be received."[14]

It seemed as if everyone across the United States was eagerly awaiting "The Puppy Episode." DeGeneres and her partner at the time, actress Anne Heche, were among them. The two had met several weeks earlier at a party after the Academy Awards. Just before the program was to be aired, the two of them and Betty DeGeneres took a limousine to a reception at the Creative Artists Agency in Los Angeles. Vance was there, too. The large group that gathered ate hors d'oeuvres and drank champagne before they settled into a nearby auditorium to watch the show.[15]

THE BIG SHOW

In the episode, the coming-out scene took place at an airport. Ellen Morgan told her friend Susan (played by Laura Dern) that she was gay. "OK. You were right," Ellen Morgan said on the show. "Susan, I'm . . . I can't. I can't even say the word. What's wrong with me? There's nothing to be ashamed of. Why am I so afraid to tell people. . . . I'm 35 years old. Why can't I just come out and say . . . I'm gay. You hear that? I'm gay. . ." During her proclamation, Ellen Morgan tripped a microphone so that her announcement was broadcast over the public-address system. The Susan character hugged her and said, "I'm so proud of you. I remember how hard it was when I told my first airport full of people."[16]

It was a long-awaited moment for fans of the show. And, it was a funny moment, too—DeGeneres was sure to inject her trademark humor into this important episode. A record 46 million people watched the show that evening in anticipation of the big announcement. "The Puppy Episode" will go down in history as the first coming out of a star character on a television sitcom. The show earned accolades, too. DeGeneres won an Emmy for writing the episode, and ABC won a Peabody Award for airing it.

Now the anticipation was over. Ellen DeGeneres was open about being gay, and the fictional Ellen Morgan had admitted it on national television. Media critics discussed

On *Ellen*, the character Ellen Morgan came out to her friend Susan at the airport, but Ellen accidentally turned on a microphone so her announcement was broadcast over the public-address system. Here, Ellen DeGeneres and Laura Dern (who played Susan) appear in that scene.

whether *Ellen* would improve with a whole new range of storylines available. But the last two shows of the 1997 season were similar to the coming-out episode: Ellen Morgan would tell her parents in one episode and her boss in the final show of the season. Some critics were disappointed at the repetitiveness of the writing, and they began to doubt that the show would survive.

Meanwhile, DeGeneres's private life became center stage as she appeared on talk shows and in the print media. Right after the show aired, Ellen, Vance, and her parents appeared on *PrimeTime Live* in separate interviews that had been recorded days before with Diane Sawyer. "When you are gay, your parents are saying how did this happen?" Ellen said during the interview. "You are a minority in your own family."[17]

Also during that interview, Ellen said that her father and his new wife asked her to move out of the house after she told them that she was gay. Elliott DeGeneres said that he did not remember that request years earlier, but he admitted that it was the wrong reaction. "If I did, I think I was wrong," he said. "It's just that simple."[18] He later added that, as he looked back through the years, he regretted his initial reaction to Ellen's being gay. He did not purposely want to hurt Ellen during this trying time in her life.

THE PERSONAL SIDE

During the interview, Diane Sawyer asked Ellen about the kind of women she liked to date, whether Ellen wanted children, and if she would campaign to make gay marriages legal. DeGeneres was unspecific about whom she dated. She said intelligence was important, as were a sense of humor and a sense of fun. She also would like someone who is independent. DeGeneres told Sawyer that she would like to have children one day but that she was not sure she would like to be pregnant, adding that she would make a good grandmother. And, she admitted that she in no way wanted to be political. "I'm not going to say 'no' to anything," DeGeneres said. "But I don't see myself campaigning for anything. . . . I don't want to be some political activist."[19]

In fact, political activist has never been a role that DeGeneres has wanted to play. When she made that statement to Sawyer, she had no idea how people would respond to *Ellen* or how the future of the sitcom would be jeopardized. As the first main character to come out on a television show, however, DeGeneres was making a political statement whether she realized it or not. Many people across the world were watching DeGeneres—she was a down-to-earth person with a keen sense of humor. People could relate to her, and the fact that she was gay seemed not to matter much at all.

Even though DeGeneres had no desire to be a gay-rights activist, the idea did not bother DeGeneres's mother. The following September, Betty DeGeneres became the spokeswoman for the largest national gay-rights political organization, the Human Rights Campaign, and its Coming Out Project. Betty DeGeneres, who was 67 years old at the time, gave her daughter a lot of support and started to give support to other parents of gay children around the world. As part of the campaign, she made personal appearances, was on television, and was featured in print advertisements. She encouraged gay people to be honest about their sexuality.[20] She created a 30-second advertisement that urged parents to give love and support to their gay children. Eventually, Betty DeGeneres also wrote a book to give other parents support.

"She's the kind of mom that gay people dream of," said Elizabeth Birch, the executive director of the Human Rights Campaign at that time. "She's a role model for parents."[21]

Betty DeGeneres was, in fact, the first straight spokesperson for the Coming Out Project. She traveled the country with her message. "The fact that I'm a mom advocating equal rights for my daughter and her partner underscores the point that ending discrimination based on sexual orientation is not just important to gay people, it's important to their families and the people who love them," she told *HRC Quarterly* in 1997.[22]

Social attitudes at the time that DeGeneres came out may have been different from what they are today. *U.S. News & World Report* reported in 1997 that a majority of people had conflicted feelings regarding homosexuality, especially concerning gay marriage and any teaching in schools that seemed to endorse homosexuality.[23] The same news magazine said that Ellen Morgan's coming out was overplayed in the media. In other words, critics thought that there was too much attention given to the coming-out episode.

Nonetheless, the show caught the attention of people all over the world. Vice President Al Gore said that it forced Americans to look at sexual orientation in a new light. A few months later, President Bill Clinton spoke at a fundraising dinner for the Human Rights Campaign. "All America

THE HUMAN RIGHTS CAMPAIGN

In 1997, just a few months after her daughter publicly announced that she was gay, Betty DeGeneres took Ellen's advice and called the Human Rights Campaign's executive director to offer her help. That year, Betty DeGeneres was named the spokesperson for the organization's Coming Out Project, a program that is designed to help gay, lesbian, bisexual, and transgender people come out and live openly.*

The Human Rights Campaign has more than 700,000 members and supporters across the country. It has a goal of achieving equality for gay, lesbian, bisexual, and transgender Americans. Founded in 1980, the organization advocates for causes that are important to the gay community.

Among its chief concerns is whether gay people can be married. The Human Rights Campaign works with state leaders across the nation to inform them of the issues surrounding gay marriage. Only in Massachusetts and Connecticut are same-sex couples entitled to all of the rights and benefits of loses if we let prejudice and discrimination stifle the hopes or deny the potential of a single American," he said. "All America loses when any person is denied or forced out of a job because of sexual orientation."[24]

At the same time all of this was happening, DeGeneres's relationship with actress Anne Heche was becoming very public. Even though their relationship was relatively new, they were getting a lot of attention. The couple was photographed at a black-tie White House Correspondents' Dinner in Washington, D.C., and at other events, too.

traditional marriages involving people of the opposite sex, as of 2008.

Same-sex marriage is a controversial topic, but it is a substantial issue for gay couples. That is partly because they would like to have the same benefits that married couples get regarding their taxes, health insurance, and survivor benefits in case one person in the relationship dies.

The HRC also provides information and support to people who want to reveal their homosexuality or bisexuality. In addition, the organization provides information and support regarding hate crimes and state laws that enable the punishment of people who commit them. The organization continues to work toward effective laws regarding hate crimes.

* "History of National Coming Out Day: 1997: Super Mom." Human Rights Campaign Web site. Available online at http://www.hrc.org/issues/3367.htm.

Ellen DeGeneres and her partner, Anne Heche, posed for photographers as they arrived at the Human Rights Campaign's national dinner in November 1997. With them was Ellen's mother, Betty DeGeneres. President Bill Clinton was the speaker at the event. DeGeneres and Heche's relationship was getting plenty of media attention.

Suddenly, even DeGeneres's private life became a public spectacle. Although both women had had relationships before this one, DeGeneres and Heche seemed convinced that theirs would go on forever. At first, they did not seem to mind the spotlight, and some publications seemed to view them as the hottest celebrity couple of the moment. Later, though, DeGeneres and Heche grew to resent being in the limelight.

By the end of 1997, it seemed, DeGeneres was more popular than ever. "I became more famous," she said, following her coming out. "So much for those people who said that it would ruin my career."[25] Still, she looked forward to getting beyond the national debate that her public coming out had generated. DeGeneres was ready to move on with her future, as an actress and a comedian and as a private person.

Unfortunately, she didn't know what was yet to come.

Another Chance

Ellen DeGeneres thought that, once she came out, the popularity of *Ellen* would grow, and she would get back to the business of being the star of a successful sitcom. The show, however, struggled, as ratings dipped. People made negative comments. *Ellen* was criticized because too many storylines focused on the fact that DeGeneres's character was gay. The network placed a parental warning before each episode, which DeGeneres complained scared off many viewers.

In an effort to promote the show, DeGeneres starred in a humorous spot that aired during *Monday Night Football*. During the ad, she told viewers, "If you enjoy watching people of the same sex pat each other on the bottom, you might want to check out my show."[1]

Even though it was meant as a joke, ABC received a million phone calls complaining about the promo. Nearly a year after DeGeneres came out, questions lingered about whether DeGeneres's show would continue on ABC. The network's advertisers and affiliates did not like its emphasis on gay storylines. "Even gay viewers are saying we're too much in-your-face," said the show's executive producer, Tim Doyle.[2]

"I'm gay, the character's gay, and that's the problem everyone has with the show," DeGeneres said in an interview with *Entertainment Tonight* in February 1998. "It's just too controversial, nobody wants to deal with it."[3]

By the spring of 1998, DeGeneres was upset by what was happening. She sensed that the show was coming to an end. ABC had not confirmed the show for the following fall season and put the show's scheduled filming on hiatus for six weeks. Eventually, the show was canceled; the last episode aired on July 22, 1998.

These decisions threw DeGeneres into a terrific depression. "Anybody who has been fired from a job—especially when you can't get another one—(knows) you go through that depression," DeGeneres told a reporter a few years later. "I didn't think I was going to be able to do anything again."[4]

In December 1998, DeGeneres and Heche announced that they had fired their agents. They were tired of being in the spotlight as gay celebrities, and they were sick of the homophobic gestures made toward them since DeGeneres publicly came out. "Everything that I ever feared happened to me," DeGeneres said. "I lost my show. I've been attacked like hell. I went from making a lot of money on a sitcom to making no money."[5] She and Heche moved to a farm outside of Los Angeles, so that they could have some privacy.[6] And DeGeneres started to try to sort out her life.

A FRESH START

Within a year, DeGeneres seemed to be re-energized. She had some movies in the works and was scheduling a stand-up tour. Her 1999 appearance in director Ron Howard's movie *EdTV*, with Matthew McConaughey, was a success, earning $22.4 million in the United States. *EdTV* was a comedy that showed some of the serious repercussions of starring in a reality television program. DeGeneres played the part of a television executive who was filming Ed's life for 24 hours. But DeGeneres's other two movies that came out around the same time—*The Love Letter* and *Goodbye Lover*—did not receive such high acclaim.

In 2000, DeGeneres scheduled a cross-country stand-up tour called The Americana Tour, which lasted nine weeks. It was the first time in seven years that she planned to travel across the country doing stand-up comedy. She struggled with writing jokes for the show, though, partly because of the cancellation of her television show. She had writer's block. "I went through three notebooks of anger and preachy stuff of what I wanted to say," she said. "And then as I wrote more and more, it went into plain ridiculous funny stories; I couldn't help myself."[7]

DeGeneres used her observational approach to comedy to talk about compassion, nature, and meditation in a humorous way. In fact, these were all issues that DeGeneres had dealt with in the time since her sitcom was canceled. She was in no mood, though, to make jokes about *Ellen*, and any political humor dealing with homosexuality was off-limits. In the end, DeGeneres said that the laughter she heard during her two-hour stand-up routine helped heal her from the turmoil she had gone through.

DeGeneres and Heche toured the country on a 45-foot customized bus, visiting more than 40 cities. At first, they loved the set-up, but after many months of touring they grew bored with it. DeGeneres was back doing what she loved the most: comedy. Still, there were times when she wondered if all of the effort was worth it.

"If I had enough money to never work again, I'd probably just work with kids and animals and eat salads at the Four Seasons, fly in a private jet maybe to an island that I owned, have a bunch of dancers that would dance for me whenever I demanded, and play Boggle," she said. "That's what I'd do."[8]

DeGeneres was tired, yet at 42 years old she would not give up. During a weeklong break from touring, she talked about the television show *Survivor* with a reporter during lunch at the Four Seasons hotel in Los Angeles. Being a survivor of a failed television show, DeGeneres seemed to see some humor in the popular new television program. "You knew that woman was going to get kicked off, but I think everybody related to that because everybody's been kicked off at some point in their life," she said. "So you know what that's like—to be the one voted out, and it's sad."[9]

Despite the disappointments, DeGeneres remained optimistic and looked toward the future. While they were

IN HER OWN WORDS

Ellen DeGeneres is known for her observational humor—her ability to mine everyday life for laughs. Here, in a blog entry from March 2008, on the Web site for her talk show, she finds the humor in something we use all the time—water:

> We pay for things that should be free. We pay for water— bottles and bottles of it. It's a lot safer than a drinking fountain. Sticking your face in the path of that geyser is always risky.

Ellen DeGeneres gave her audience the thumbs-up during a stop in 2000 on her nine-week Americana Tour. It was her first stand-up tour in seven years. DeGeneres was trying to pick up the pieces after the disappointment of the cancellation of her sitcom in 1998.

on the tour, Heche filmed a behind-the-scenes documentary. In addition, DeGeneres's performance at the Beacon Theatre in New York was recorded and scheduled to appear on HBO the following July. The one-hour program was called *Ellen DeGeneres: The Beginning*. DeGeneres decided to mention the gay issue early in the performance just to get it out of the way; she followed with a dance routine. "Ultimately, I decided I don't want to talk about it," she said during the performance. "I feel it would be best expressed through interpretive dance."[10] She told a reporter that she wanted to get to the point where she was considered "the artist formerly known as a lesbian."[11]

Comedy was, in fact, DeGeneres's first love, and she would continue to work hard to see if she could again become a success. The reviews of her stand-up shows throughout the United States were very good. "You can see the comedy in each of her stories, because they are not only so goofy and meandering, but also full of imagery and description," a reviewer for the *Chicago Tribune* wrote. "And you can't help but chuckle at the sights she creates."[12]

NO REGRETS

If DeGeneres had any doubts about still being funny, after becoming the gay political icon many saw her as, she was wrong. The critics agreed: Ellen DeGeneres was still hilarious. And, DeGeneres had no regrets about choosing to go public with her homosexuality. "It's the best thing I ever did for myself," she said a few years later. "It certainly was a bad thing for my career for a while, and that hurt my feelings in many ways. But once all that settled, I'm able to be exactly who I am and I have nothing to hide anymore."[13]

DeGeneres and Heche were involved in another HBO special that was shown for the first time in 2000. *If These Walls Could Talk 2* featured a trilogy of stories about lesbianism. DeGeneres served as executive producer, and

Heche wrote and directed the third segment of the trilogy. (Abortion was the first topic tackled by *If These Walls Could Talk* four years earlier.) DeGeneres was joined by actresses Vanessa Redgrave, Sharon Stone, Michelle Williams, and Chloë Sevigny, among others. In the third segment of *If These Walls Could Talk 2*, DeGeneres and Stone were featured in a romantic comedy about a lesbian couple trying to have a baby with the help of a sperm donor.[14]

One of the few times that DeGeneres talked about the politics of being gay was when she appeared on *Larry King Live* to promote that HBO special. "Do you want to marry?" Larry King asked her and Heche, who was also appearing on the show. "Yes," DeGeneres said. The three of them proceeded to discuss the fact that gay marriage was illegal in the United States.[15] (As of 2008, gay marriage was legalized in Massachusetts and Connectictut.) Even though many gay activists across the United States lobby their state legislators for the right to marry, DeGeneres has never been too outspoken on the issue.

The politics involved with being gay have never been DeGeneres's highest priority. At this time in her life, she simply was trying hard to move forward with her career. "I felt like people hated me because I wasn't getting work," she told Larry King during a later interview on CNN. "The phone stopped ringing, and nobody was interested in anything to do with me."[16] Around the same time, her personal life suffered another terrific blow. Heche literally walked out of their isolated home and was briefly hospitalized. After three-and-a-half years together, DeGeneres and Heche's relationship had ended—their very public breakup splashed across the media. Heche married a cameraman who had been involved with her HBO documentary, and the two of them had a child soon after that.[17]

Although DeGeneres was devastated by Heche's departure, she moved ahead with her life. Eventually, she met a

31-year-old photographer named Alexandra Hedison, with whom she lived in Beverly Hills with their two cats and two dogs. (DeGeneres had sold the home where she and Heche lived near Ojai, California.)

A DELICATE HOSTING JOB

In 2001, DeGeneres was asked to host the fifty-third Emmy Awards—however, unusual circumstances surrounded the production. Scheduled for September 18, the awards ceremony was first postponed because of the September 11 terrorist attacks on the World Trade Center and the Pentagon. DeGeneres's initial script for the show was thrown away after the attacks.

When the Emmy Awards were rescheduled, DeGeneres made an attempt at writing a more serious script in the light of the attacks. But, that second show was also canceled, as the U.S. war on terrorism began in Afghanistan. Finally, on the third attempt, the show was aired on November 4— but not without increased security due to the attacks. DeGeneres recalled bomb-sniffing dogs going through her dressing room. She knew that sharpshooters were planted around the building and that executives were very nervous that a room full of celebrities would be an easy target for terrorists.[18]

Although she had worn a dress for the 1994 Emmy Awards, DeGeneres chose a dark pantsuit to open the 2001 ceremony. Onstage, she joked about the entertainment industry, terrorists, and other topics. "What could bug the Taliban more than seeing a gay woman in a suit surrounded by Jews?" she joked in a politically incorrect sense during the telecast.[19] DeGeneres received a standing ovation from the crowd.

Meanwhile, DeGeneres started to get more calls about work. CBS had offered her an opportunity to film six episodes of a series called *The Ellen Show*, which would have the

Hey, she sort of wore a dress again. During the 2001 Emmy Awards, Ellen DeGeneres spoofed the singer Björk, who had worn a swan dress to the Academy Awards that year. After the terrorist attacks of September 11, 2001, the Emmy Awards ceremony was canceled twice. DeGeneres won wide acclaim for her understated tone in hosting the ceremony.

feel of a classic variety show.[20] By the time the show aired in September 2001, it had become a sitcom. DeGeneres played Ellen Richmond, a former Internet executive who moved back to her small hometown. The character was a lesbian, but her sexuality was not the focus. Only 13 episodes of *The Ellen Show* were shown before CBS canceled the program. By now, DeGeneres was wondering if she would ever have a popular television show again.

In the summer of 2002, the publishing giant Simon & Schuster announced that DeGeneres would write a book of comic essays. "Ellen's ingenious wit was meant for the page," said Rob Weisbach, a vice president at Simon & Schuster, who was looking forward to reading DeGeneres's work. "And how lucky am I? Most people don't get to be entertained by the funniest woman on the planet while they work."[21]

Despite the end of her second sitcom, DeGeneres continued to work on other projects. She hosted *Saturday Night Live*'s Christmas special and was also a guest celebrity on *Hollywood Squares*. In the spring of 2003, she launched a 35-city tour, called the Here and Now tour, which was also featured in an HBO special.[22]

One of DeGeneres's greatest movie credits occurred later that summer. She was a hit as the voice of the animated fish, Dory, in *Finding Nemo*. DeGeneres was surprised by the acclaim she received as Dory as well as the popularity of *Finding Nemo*, which became the highest-grossing animated film of all time—earning $860 million worldwide. "Nothing was going on, and I hadn't reached a confident place yet," she said. "I hate to sound fatalistic, but that's where I was."[23] *Finding Nemo* won Best Animated Feature Film during the 2004 Academy Awards. Through all of this, DeGeneres was fond of the fish. "I got to love that Dory has memory loss," she said. "It makes her so innocent and optimistic. Having such a limited attention span makes her so childlike."[24]

One of the movie's writers and directors, though, wasn't a bit surprised at the film's success. A longtime fan of DeGeneres's, Andrew Stanton said that the movie had done so well largely because of her. "Everybody has that friend who's funny merely for existing," Stanton said. "That's Ellen. You're not waiting for a punch line with her. You're just waiting for her to speak so you can start laughing."[25]

Things were starting to happen again for the hard-working DeGeneres. Her 2001 performance at the twice-delayed Emmy Awards seemed to have left a mark. "That was the turning point," said Jim Paratore, who was president of Telepictures, a television syndication company. "Ellen came out there and made people proud. People began to step back and remember how talented she was. And talent, over time, wins out in this business."[26]

Paratore was the man who would tap DeGeneres's talent next, leading to another great success.

Movin' and
Groovin' on TV

Ellen DeGeneres was relaxing on the huge, brown sofa in her NBC Studio office in Burbank, California. It was just days before *The Ellen DeGeneres Show* was set to air, and she was being interviewed by a reporter from *Entertainment Weekly*. On a wall above DeGeneres's desk hung a framed photo of Oprah Winfrey taken during Winfrey's guest appearance on *Ellen*'s coming-out show. "Oprah is amazing," DeGeneres told the reporter. "And, I thought it was pretty impressive that now, here I am doing a talk show."[1]

DeGeneres was in a light-hearted mood, and it was reflected during the conversation. Her trademark humor was evident, this time involving facts about the natural world. "There's a species of caterpillar that looks like bird droppings, all so that birds won't eat it. How amazing is it that nature knows what it looks like from a distance, and turns itself into something that looks like a bird dropping?" she asked the reporter. "Oh, sorry," she added. "I don't think I'm being particularly funny today."[2]

After several years of wondering if her television comedy career was over, DeGeneres was back and she was excited about her new talk show. It was scheduled to begin on September 8, 2003, and the pressure was on. DeGeneres was a bit stressed out—she would need to come up with funny monologues for each show and figure out how to entertain her audience for an hour each day. "I've been interested in doing a talk show for a long time," she said. "I'll do a monologue and talk to the audience, but the rest we still have to figure out. I have to stay true to what I am."[3]

Even though she was perfectly comfortable as a comedian, the idea of doing a funny, 10-minute monologue every day intimidated DeGeneres. "It's real pressure to find something funny every day," she said. "I mean, I'll look at a chair or a rug and think, there are people who make rugs—and that turns into something. I try to notice every single thing now and go beyond it."[4]

ENTERTAINMENT, NOT POLITICS

One thing was certain: DeGeneres's talk show would not focus on her relationships or her sexuality. Nor would it focus on political issues surrounding gay marriage and such. Jim Paratore, of Telepictures, had told DeGeneres: "The audience doesn't want to hear Oprah preach spirituality. They didn't want to hear Rosie (O'Donnell) preach gun control. And they don't want to hear you preach lifestyle."[5]

DeGeneres agreed. Even though she had no regrets, she felt that she had learned a hard lesson in show business with *Ellen*'s "The Puppy Episode." By tackling the controversial topic of homosexuality, she had risked the show's support from advertisers, viewers, and network executives. She decided that she would be careful about that this time.

Her show would not be a platform to discuss her personal life, although at the time she said that she might talk about what she did the night before or what was going on at her home. Still, her monologues would probably go no further than that. "It's not my job to get into an argument with somebody about religion or politics or sexuality or anything," she said. "It is my job to make people laugh."[6]

But over and over again, it seemed, DeGeneres had to reassure everyone that she would not focus on her sexuality. "Are you going to talk about being gay?" Matt Lauer asked during an interview on the *Today* show on the morning of September 8. "Oh, I haven't talked about that for a long time," DeGeneres responded.[7] *The Ellen DeGeneres Show* was set to debut that afternoon.

In the months spent planning her show, DeGeneres knew only that she wanted it to be fun. She decided that she would invite a mix of celebrities as well as ordinary people to be her guests. She hired a disc jockey to provide music during the program. Little did she know that the music would inspire her and her audience to new heights of talk-show exuberance.

During the planning process, DeGeneres also thought about Johnny Carson, the comedian whose show she appeared on so many years ago. She liked Carson's relaxed and funny conversations with the guests who appeared on his late-night program, and she hoped that she would be able to copy that style.

DeGeneres also liked another popular talk-show host, Oprah Winfrey. Even though Winfrey is not a comedian, DeGeneres admired how Winfrey casually interviewed her guests and how her show drew in so many viewers. In many television markets, DeGeneres's show would be on at the same time as Winfrey's show. DeGeneres joked about the situation with Matt Lauer. "Yeah. Yeah. It's hard," DeGeneres said. "She's established a following. . . . If we wrestled, I'd win."[8] It was intimidating for DeGeneres to go up against the most popular daytime talk show of the time.

DeGeneres also knew that the audience for a daytime talk show would be different from what it was for her evening sitcoms, and she tried to figure out what would appeal to those who watched television during the day—including some children and retired folks. "I'm going to talk to people and have a conversation with people and hopefully ask different kinds of questions than other talk shows," she decided. "I'll try to do something different and have it be a happy, positive show every day."[9]

During interviews with reporters, DeGeneres was continually asked about all of the past celebrities who had hosted talk shows that failed. DeGeneres was undaunted, though. She was confident that her show would work. "I have never been so passionate about something," she said. "I will probably do this for the rest of my career."[10]

Indeed, the talk show sounded as though it could be a good fit for DeGeneres. "She is funny, she's quirky, and she has a brand-new TV show," announced Matt Lauer, as he introduced DeGeneres on *Today*. After they talked about DeGeneres's excitement and how she planned to avoid politics, Lauer asked if Betty DeGeneres, who had become an outspoken activist on gay issues since Ellen's public coming out, would appear on the show.[11]

"My mom's there every single day. . . . I can't get rid of her," DeGeneres joked, regarding her mother's habit of sitting in while the shows were being taped. "I mean, my mom and I are really close . . . and she's in L.A., so she comes to the show every day."[12]

DeGeneres was excited about what her future would bring. Perhaps in anticipation of all the trips to the

Jennifer Aniston was the first guest on *The Ellen DeGeneres Show* when it debuted in September 2003. The talk show seemed to be a perfect fit for DeGeneres. "I have never been so passionate about something," she said. "I will probably do this for the rest of my career."

NBC studio over the coming years, she bought a contemporary style home on three acres in the hills above Hollywood. She and Hedison lived there, surrounded by three ponds and lots of wildlife. "I've moved a lot," DeGeneres said, "and I hope I don't ever move again."[13]

A FAN FAVORITE

Once again, DeGeneres's popularity began to blossom. Her talk show started to attract more and more viewers. DeGeneres's second book, *The Funny Thing Is . . .* , was published in 2003, and it was a huge success, hitting *The New York Times* best-seller list.

"I don't consider myself a writer. . . . I would never have thought I'd write one book, much less two books," she said during an interview on National Public Radio. While promoting her book, DeGeneres peppered the interview with a few humorous observations. "The more that modern technology tries to help us, it actually ends up hurting us," DeGeneres said. "And the fact that people are trying to get more tissue by making it thinner is not helping anybody. . . . When the tissue is that thin, and especially in a public bathroom where the wheel—it's like a cheese-wheel size of toilet paper that just rips every two inches, I think that we're in big trouble in this country, I tell you."[14]

It seems as if DeGeneres should have been running out of jokes by now, but she still came up with plenty of funny observations. She became very comfortable with the monologue at the beginning of each show. She taped her show four days a week. (The fifth show of each week was shot on an earlier day or was a rerun.) DeGeneres loved the work, despite its challenges. "It's the hardest job I've ever had, but it's the most satisfaction I've ever had, so I'm sure it's like being a mother," she told a reporter for *People* in 2005. "It challenges you every day."[15]

Yet, anyone watching DeGeneres's show would think that the star was very relaxed. She seemed to find some comfort in dancing every day—a programming decision that boosted her popularity among people of all ages. "I didn't want a band," DeGeneres said. "I wanted a D.J., and I love music. And so I had a D.J. and when I finish my monologue, I come out and do basically a little bit of stand-up. . . . When I go to sit down, there's music playing and I like to dance, so I dance. It started as a joke. Then I started dancing more and then suddenly the audience started standing up and dancing with me. Now, it's a major part of the show where I dance in the beginning and it's a huge thing."[16]

DeGeneres was enjoying her newfound success. On her show, she was known for wearing neat, button-down shirts with vests or jackets and one of her many pairs of Vans. She was having so much fun, it seemed, that she was no longer concerned about competing in the same time slot as Winfrey. In fact, she joked about the top-rated talk-show host with a reporter from *People*. "I just think that she should retire," she said. "I mean, Oprah, take a rest! Go and relax and enjoy your life!"[17]

Among DeGeneres's fans was one of her favorite come-dians, Bob Newhart. "DeGeneres is the bravest and most honest female comedian I have ever seen work because she publicly announced she's gay," Newhart once wrote. "That revelation could have ended her career, as she had to be aware, but she also knew she had to be honest."[18]

At the same time, DeGeneres seemed very content in her personal life. She started to do some print and television advertisements for American Express, which featured DeGeneres with animals. By 2005, she and Hedison had broken up, and DeGeneres had found a new love, actress Portia de Rossi, with whom she lived in Los Angeles with a few cats that they had rescued. DeGeneres's humor was

DID YOU KNOW?

Although Ellen DeGeneres loves to dance to hip-hop on her talk show, she listens to classic rock—like the Doobie Brothers or Led Zeppelin—when she's driving. And she says that any song by Rush would be her favorite karaoke song.

reflected in the cat's names: Charlie, George Jackson, and Chairman Meow Tse-Tung. "This is my priority," DeGeneres told a reporter. "If everything else went away,

OPRAH WINFREY

As *The Ellen DeGeneres Show* grew in popularity, DeGeneres would make good-natured comments about Oprah Winfrey's plans for retirement. Then, in the early part of 2008, the Harris Poll's annual list of favorite television stars showed that DeGeneres, in fact, was starting to eclipse Winfrey's popularity. As DeGeneres took the No. 1 spot, Winfrey moved down to No. 2.

But that is where the comparisons between the two women end. Winfrey's path to daytime success was much different from DeGeneres's. DeGeneres is a comedian, and Winfrey— even though she can easily make her audience laugh—is not. Winfrey's success did not come from her ability to make people laugh but from her skills at sitting down on national television and having a heartfelt discussion with a range of guests.

Oprah Gail Winfrey was born to an extremely poor, unmarried woman in Kosciusko, Mississippi, on January 29, 1954. Her mother was only 18 years old, and her father, who was in the Army, did not even know that he had fathered a child until a birth announcement arrived in the mail asking him to send clothes.*

As she was growing up, Winfrey lived mainly with her poor grandparents. Even though they had no money, and Winfrey often went without shoes, her grandmother became her greatest supporter. She convinced Winfrey that she could be anything that she wanted.

Eventually, Winfrey met her father and moved to Nashville to live with him and his wife. But her life was shaped by her as long as I've saved enough money that I can live with trees and animals around, that's the most important thing to me.[19]

actions as a teen—before she lived with her father, Winfrey gave birth at the age of 14 to a baby who died just a few days later. It was a story that was not told until many decades later when her daytime talk show was at the height of its popularity.

Winfrey's life got back on track. By the time she graduated from high school, she was interested in a broadcasting career and was a newsreader at a Nashville television station. Winfrey continued to work at the television station, and at the age of 19, she became the youngest news anchor in Nashville. By the time she was 22, she was working at a television station in Baltimore, Maryland. Winfrey struggled to hide her emotions while on camera, and that was a challenge for television news. Her true talents did not show through until a few years later, when she became a co-host of a popular local program called *People Are Talking*.

After seven years in Baltimore, Winfrey went to a Chicago television station to work on a program called *A.M. Chicago*. By the end of its first month, with Winfrey at the helm, the show became the top-rated program in the area. At the end of its first season, the show's name was changed to *The Oprah Winfrey Show*—and its popularity began to eclipse that of the top talk-show host of the time: a man by the name of Phil Donahue.

---

*Sherry Beck Paprocki. *Oprah Winfrey: Talk Show Host and Media Magnate*. New York: Chelsea House Publishers, 2006, p. 9.

DeGeneres and de Rossi also purchased a large house just outside of Los Angeles in Montecito, California, near a home owned by Winfrey. The house had four bedrooms, eight bathrooms, a pool, a tennis court, and sweeping views of the mountains and ocean. In her spare time, DeGeneres watched *Animal Planet* while exercising on her elliptical machine. And, she was learning to ride her new horse named Puff.

Certainly, DeGeneres had to stay in shape to do all the dancing she did on her show. Apparently, she had no plans to stop, either. "When I'm 80, I'm going to be dancing with my walker," she said. "What's great is that there's no one way to dance. And that's kind of my philosophy about everything."[20]

It was a fact, of course, that few other stars had achieved the success that DeGeneres had without formal training of any kind. For DeGeneres, it was important that she was creative in the way she styled her career—she was not only a comedian, but also a successful actress, a writer, and now a talk-show host. DeGeneres's patience and perseverance through every obstacle she had encountered had led her to the place where she was today. No other person could take the credit for her success, other than the star herself.

DeGeneres's show was successful, and she seemed to have no trouble attracting celebrity guests. Jennifer Aniston, Denise Richards, Charlie Sheen, Cameron Diaz, and others agreed to appear. Media critics speculated that it was because DeGeneres did not ask embarrassing questions, partly because she had been in similar situations herself. "I think they trust me," DeGeneres said. "I think everyone knows that I'm not going to make anyone feel uncomfortable. That's not who I am as a person. I never use someone as the punch line of a joke."[21]

DeGeneres was enjoying her success, as she was still in the position to make great strides for women. When a

Ellen DeGeneres and her new partner, Portia de Rossi, posed for the cameras when they arrived at the Daytime Emmy Awards in May 2005 in New York City. Since her talk show's debut in 2003, DeGeneres and the program have won several Daytime Emmy Awards.

reporter asked her if she would ever consider being a late-night talk-show host, DeGeneres responded with enthusiasm. "Of course I'd do late night," she said. "It would be a great challenge because there hasn't really been a successful woman on late night. But I seem to be doing fine now, so we'll see what happens."[22]

In 2005, she once again hosted the Primetime Emmy Awards. By this point in her career, DeGeneres was intimately familiar with the various awards program. In 2004, her show was nominated for 12 Daytime Emmy Awards. DeGeneres even found humor in the 12 nominations, as she joked that she was disappointed that the show was not nominated in the Best Song category. "I'm like, I want everything," she laughed.[23] When the winners were announced, the show won four awards, including Outstanding Talk Show.

By 2005, DeGeneres was becoming famous with other celebrities for her dance moves. When she appeared on the *Today* show with Katie Couric, both women danced. "Come on, Katie," DeGeneres said. "You don't dance enough. You could dance on this show."[24] Couric was embarrassed and stopped soon after she started. She talked to DeGeneres about her show's success. "It's just positive energy, which I think everybody's looking for these days," DeGeneres said.[25]

DeGeneres stopped by the *Today* show while she was in New York to tape several segments for her own program. One day, she danced on the floor of the New York Stock Exchange. "They started clanking things together to force me to dance," she said, amazed at the response from the stockbrokers who worked there.[26] Another New York show featured DeGeneres sliding down a fire pole at a firehouse in the Bronx. "Let me tell you," she said, "the firemen—fire people—don't get enough credit for going down that pole alone."[27]

Also in 2005, DeGeneres was nominated for a Grammy Award for Best Comedy Album, which was the audio version of her book *The Funny Thing Is. . . .* And, she won more Daytime Emmy Awards—five in 2005 and six in 2006, including Outstanding Talk Show and Outstanding Talk Show Host both years.

During an interview with a writer from *In Style* magazine in 2005, DeGeneres confessed that her favorite place to people-watch was at Central Park in New York City. In addition, she said that her favorite dessert was an occasional indulgence of Häagen-Dazs coffee ice cream. And, despite years of being somewhat uninterested in fashion, DeGeneres appeared to be developing some specific tastes in clothes, too. She liked to shop at Barneys, she said, and she loved the brands of Jil Sander, Helmut Lang, Prada, and Gucci. "People think I don't get into fashion because I dress a certain way on the show, but I love clothes," she said.[28]

A STARTLING EVENT

Just days before her show was to begin its third season in 2005, DeGeneres and many other people across the United States were stunned by the news that her hometown of New Orleans, along with the southern coasts of Mississippi and other surrounding states, was devastated by Hurricane Katrina.

"I'm from New Orleans so my family (has moved to) Mississippi, and they've lost everything, and my friends have lost everything. . . . And now I just feel numb," she told a reporter on CBS's *The Saturday Early Show* just a few days after the storm hit.[29] DeGeneres reported that an aunt once lost a house during a hurricane and it had been rebuilt. Hurricane Katrina, however, destroyed the property again, and all that her aunt had were four pictures that she took on her way out and four pieces of silverware that were found after the storm.

Being from New Orleans, DeGeneres had plenty of memories of her father boarding up their houses to prepare for a hurricane strike. Still, she had never seen such devastation as that caused by the most recent storm. Like Americans across the country, in horror, she watched the television images showing people who had become homeless and hungry after the storm, along with the landscapes that had become flattened when houses blew away. She was appalled at the slow response to send help, and she immediately planned to take part in a telethon that was scheduled for the following Friday night to help raise funds for residents of the area.

When she had taped her first show of the season, DeGeneres could not bring herself to do her usual comedic monologue. "I talked about my family and my friends, and I cried and tried not to cry," she said. "I just don't want to ignore that fact that something horrible is going on and that a million people are homeless and jobless, you know. It's too big to ignore, but at the same time, my job is to make people forget, you know."[30]

A few weeks later, DeGeneres hosted the Primetime Emmy Awards—oddly enough, once again, she was hosting an awards program following a devastating national event. "This is the second time I've hosted the Emmys after a national tragedy," she said during her monologue, "and I just want to say that I'm honored because it's times like this that we really, really need laughter."[31]

DeGeneres continued her work to help the residents of New Orleans. Throughout the fall, her show's Hurricane Katrina Relief Fund raised nearly $10 million for the American Red Cross. The following January, DeGeneres's show teamed up with the Quiznos chain to give away a restaurant to a local resident interested in owning a franchise. "There's really no one else in the country who can touch the lives of so many people with her wonderful gift

Ellen DeGeneres surveyed the work that still needed to be done in the Lower Ninth Ward of New Orleans following Hurricane Katrina. Her visit, in May 2006, came eight months after the hurricane devastated the Louisiana city. DeGeneres was raising millions of dollars through her talk show to help the relief effort.

of laughter even during the most difficult times," Quiznos' chief executive officer, Rick Schaden, said.[32]

A few months later, DeGeneres went to New Orleans for the first time since Katrina had hit. She was there to help open the new Quiznos restaurant, which was won by a local resident whose home and grocery store were ruined in the floods that followed the hurricane. "Rebuild New Orleans, rebuild New Orleans, rebuild New Orleans," DeGeneres shouted into a bullhorn as those standing around her joined in.[33]

(continues on page 98)

HURRICANE KATRINA

Hurricane Katrina struck New Orleans on August 29, 2005. A few hours later, one of America's most unique cities was inundated with water as massive flooding occurred. Ellen DeGeneres was joined by the rest of the world as she watched televised reports of the disaster in her hometown.

Hurricane Katrina is considered by many people to be the greatest natural disaster ever to hit the United States. More than 140 square miles in New Orleans were flooded when levees—which were built to protect the city against such disasters—failed. The floodwaters covered much of the city for more than six weeks.

More than 1,460 residents of Louisiana died, and more than 160,000 homes were destroyed or damaged throughout the city. More than two years later, many of the 240,000 evacuees had yet to return. Some had found homes in other parts of the country. Other residents were still homeless, living in tents under bridges or in temporary trailers where their homes once stood.*

One of the poorest sections of the city, called the Lower Ninth Ward, was devastated when the levees failed. Houses in the Lower Ninth Ward—one of the most historically and culturally rich neighborhoods of the United States—were torn off their foundations and floated in the floodwaters. Nearly four weeks later, the Louisiana and Mississippi coasts were hit again by a milder storm called Hurricane Rita. On top of the destruction caused by Katrina, Rita was considered just one more blow.

As people around the country watched the aftermath of the disasters, DeGeneres overcame the shock that she felt and went into action. Her show's Hurricane Katrina Relief Fund raised nearly $10 million for the American Red Cross. At Christmas in 2005, DeGeneres's Toys for Tots drive raised nearly $1 million for the children who were displaced. But, for DeGeneres, her help had only just begun. Like others, she questioned why the city's rebuilding process was taking so long.

In December 2006, actor Brad Pitt decided to create the Make It Right Project, to focus on rebuilding homes for victims of Katrina.** He developed a goal of rebuilding housing that was safe, healthy, and environmentally friendly. The Make It Right Project is striving to rebuild 150 homes in the Lower Ninth Ward. To launch the project, Pitt led an effort to build a community of pink fabric houses—this was an effort to raise awareness around the world that help was still needed.

DeGeneres liked the idea. She began to raise funds on *The Ellen DeGeneres Show* to assist Pitt with the project. By early 2008, DeGeneres's viewers had contributed more than $1 million to build nearly seven homes. The fundraising continued: DeGeneres requested donations to Pitt's organization in honor of her fiftieth birthday. On January 26, 2008, it had been 50 years since DeGeneres was born in a hospital near New Orleans.

---

*Bruce Nolan, "Remembering Katrina," *The New Orleans Times-Picayune.* August 29, 2006.
**"The MIR Project." Available online at http://www.makeitrightnola.org.

(continued from page 95)

DeGeneres was sad when she saw how much work still needed to be done in the city. It had been months since the storm, but debris was still piled along sidewalks, and thousands of homes were uninhabitable. Some had no electricity or other services, such as water and sewage. "People are not taking this seriously," DeGeneres complained. "It's not OK for this to be happening in this country."[34] During the same visit, DeGeneres planned to have dinner with former U.S. Presidents George H.W. Bush and Bill Clinton, who were in New Orleans to raise funds to assist the clean-up effort. On the spur of the moment, a few days later, she participated in the graduation ceremony for Tulane University at New Orleans Arena, located near the Superdome.

The official commencement speakers were the two former presidents, who had raised more than $130 million for the Bush-Clinton Katrina Fund.[35] DeGeneres was the one who made the crowd laugh. "I heard everyone should be wearing robes," she joked as she wore a white bathrobe and slippers onstage. "Seriously," she added, "you are amazing people. . . . To get this far and all of the sudden get displaced and have to go to different schools—it's an experience that will form you, shape you, mold you and, suddenly, you're Jell-O."[36]

DeGeneres continued to talk to the graduates, instinctively knowing that laughter would be good for these students who had experienced a very difficult year. "Take care of yourselves," she told them. "When you're younger, you don't listen to your parents, so I really want to say it: hydrate, exfoliate, moisturize, exercise, and floss!"[37]

After that, the Tulane president handed DeGeneres a fringed umbrella and the two of them danced off the stage to jazz music being played by a local band.

More Than a
Comedian

Ellen DeGeneres has focused on being funny with the hope that her humor would make other people laugh. She has persevered through many challenges—her parents' divorce, the abuse by her stepfather, the many peaks and valleys in her career as a comedian and actress, and coming out as a gay woman. Sure, DeGeneres has had much good fortune—her first sitcom was considered successful until after the coming-out episode. But then, DeGeneres entered one of the most depressing periods in her adult life. She worried that her career was over—and even went back out on the road to do a grueling stand-up tour across the country.

At the beginning of 2007, DeGeneres realized one of the biggest goals in her life. She was invited to host the 79th Academy Awards at the Kodak Theatre in Los Angeles. She was thrilled despite the hard work it would take to prepare for the live event, which frequently lasts more than three hours.

"Ellen DeGeneres was born to host the Academy Awards," the show's producer, Laura Ziskin, said. "There is no more challenging hosting job in show business. It requires someone who can keep the show alive and fresh and moving, as well as someone who is a flat-out great entertainer. Ellen completely fits the bill."[1]

DeGeneres responded with her typical humor. "There's two things I've always wanted to do in my life," she said. "One is to host the Oscars. The second is to get a call from Laura Ziskin. You can imagine that day's diary entry."[2]

DeGeneres was only the second woman ever invited to host the awards. Actress Whoopi Goldberg was the first and had done it four times, most recently in 2002. Those involved with the Academy expressed great confidence in DeGeneres's abilities.

She had many fans affiliated with the prominent award show. "She just sparkles," said Sid Ganis, the president of the Academy of Motion Picture Arts and Sciences. "She is such a pleasure to watch. Her wit cuts to the truth of things, but in a wonderfully warm-spirited way. I think she'll be a fantastic host for this show, and we're extremely pleased that she's agreed to do it."[3]

One reporter asked DeGeneres who her favorite Academy Awards host had been through the years. DeGeneres remembered admiring Johnny Carson—the late-night talk-show host whose show she first appeared on. "He had a classiness about him that I was drawn to," she said. "He just made you feel good watching him. And it had nothing to do with if he was the funniest. You were in good hands when he walked out."[4]

In a funny moment during the 2007 Academy Awards ceremony, Ellen DeGeneres asked director Steven Spielberg *(right)* to take a picture of her and actor/director Clint Eastwood. DeGeneres was only the second woman ever to host the Academy Awards.

It had now been 10 years since DeGeneres's coming-out episode on her first sitcom. And, it seemed, she was widely accepted by those at the Academy Awards as well as viewers throughout the country. "It's remarkable how unremarkable it is that a gay person is hosting the Oscars," James Poniewozik wrote in *Time* magazine.[5]

Certainly, DeGeneres's role in the awards show affected a few things that evening. Gay performer Melissa Etheridge took the opportunity to thank her "wife" when she accepted an award for Best Original Song for "I Need to Wake Up,"

(continues on page 104)

THE AWARDS SHOWS

Ellen DeGeneres is an award-winning celebrity who has also hosted many of television's top award programs. Through 2008, *The Ellen DeGeneres Show* had won 25 Daytime Emmy Awards. In addition, DeGeneres has won numerous other awards, including two People's Choice Awards and the Johnny Carson Producer of the Year Award in Variety Television, which is given by the Producers Guild.

Sometimes it is challenging to sort out which awards honor which programs. That may especially be the case with DeGeneres, who has also hosted some of the entertainment industry's leading award programs. In fact, DeGeneres has received awards for her work hosting other awards programs.

Here is a quick glance at the highest-profile awards in the industry and DeGeneres's relationship to them:

- **Academy Awards:** In 2007, DeGeneres was the second woman ever invited to host the Academy Awards. (Whoopi Goldberg hosted four shows before that.) The Academy Awards are given out by the Academy of Motion Picture Arts and Sciences, an organization that includes more than 6,000 motion-picture artists and craftspeople. DeGeneres has never won an Academy Award; therefore, she has never taken home the small statue that the winners receive, called the Oscar. However, *Finding Nemo*, a film in which DeGeneres did the voice of the fish Dory, won the Oscar for Best Animated Feature Film in 2004.

- **Emmy Awards:** The Academy of Television Arts and Sciences honors prime-time television programming, while the National Academy of Television Arts and Sciences honors daytime, sports, news, and documentary programs. DeGeneres's talk show has won 25 Daytime Emmy Awards. In 1997, DeGeneres won a Primetime Emmy for writing "The Puppy Episode" for *Ellen*.

- **Grammy Awards:** The Grammy Awards are presented by The Recording Academy and are the only peer-presented awards that honor artistic achievement, technical proficiency, and overall excellence in the recording industry. DeGeneres hosted the Grammy Awards in 1996 and 1997. In 2005, the audio version of her second book was nominated for a Grammy Award.

- **Peabody Awards:** DeGeneres's coming-out episode on her sitcom earned a George Foster Peabody Award. The Peabody Awards are presented annually by the Grady College of Journalism and Mass Communication at the University of Georgia. George Foster Peabody was a successful investment banker from Columbus, Georgia, who devoted much of his fortune to education and social enterprise.

- **Johnny Carson Producer of the Year Award in Variety Television:** This award is presented by the Producers Guild of America, a nonprofit organization that represents more than 1,600 motion-picture, television, and new media producers. DeGeneres won this award in 2005 and 2006 for her work as a producer on *The Ellen DeGeneres Show*.

- **People's Choice Awards:** Created in 1975, these awards are a result of fans voting for their favorite performers, TV shows, and movies. Four times DeGeneres has been named the Favorite Funny Female Star and Favorite Daytime Talk Show Host.

(continued from page 101)

which she created for the film *An Inconvenient Truth*. "Well, I think the Oscars are like, it's like a gay holiday," Etheridge said during a backstage interview. "It's a real mix of lots of different diversities here tonight. And I'm grateful to be part of that."[6]

After the awards, DeGeneres got great reviews. "I can't remember an Oscars that radiated such good vibes," raved a reviewer from *Newsweek*. "Other hosts may have been funnier, and edgier, but none created more relaxed goodwill in the hall: she wasn't competing with the celebrities in attendance, and her low-key humor removed any taint of self-importance from the evening."[7]

After the Academy Awards, it seemed that DeGeneres's talk show grew even more popular. Still, though, there were challenging situations. One such situation involved a dog—a Brussels Griffon mix named Iggy—that she and de Rossi had adopted in September 2007. But the rescue organization from which they had adopted the dog requested that it be returned because DeGeneres had given it to her hairdresser's family. DeGeneres was terribly upset.

"I love animals," she said during her monologue on the show on that September day. This was one of the few times that DeGeneres found it impossible to be funny during the opening segment. "I love animals," she said again. "I rescue them and I've adopted so many animals and found so many animals homes over the years. On September 20, I adopted a dog from a rescue organization here in the area. I got it neutered. I got it trained, and I paid my vet extra money to take it home to sleep in the bed with him at night instead of a cage. I spent $3,000 on this puppy to acclimate it, to train it to be with our cats. It was just too much energy and too rambunctious."[8]

So, DeGeneres decided to give the dog to her hairdresser's family. The rescue organization, though, took the dog away from them after discovering that. DeGeneres begged that the dog be returned to the family—the media covered the story in great detail after DeGeneres cried during her show and dozens of bloggers responded on DeGeneres's Web site. DeGeneres was so upset, she canceled the taping of her show a few days later. This on-air breakdown caused a blogger from *The Washington Post* to make fun of her emotional state.[9] For a few brief days, it seemed that DeGeneres was once again on the hot seat for something that she had done in her personal life.

Within weeks, though, DeGeneres was back to her usual banter during her talk show. Dancing continued to play a large part on the program. "Happiness makes you dance," she wrote on her Web site in November 2007. "Music makes you feel so much, and when you can't contain it any more, you have to express it with your body. It's like joy erupting out of you. It's the only emotion that triggers dancing."[10]

THE FOUR-LEGGEDS' FRIEND

Even after the Iggy incident, DeGeneres continued to be dedicated to her lifelong love of animals. She had come a long way from the early 1990s, when she was a regular viewer of the Discovery Channel and a fan of naturalists Dian Fossey and Jane Goodall.

Now, with a successful talk show, she was able to lure guests like emeritus zoo director Jack Hanna from Columbus, Ohio, who brought rare and unusual animals for DeGeneres and her audience to enjoy. In early 2008, she announced that she had become a partner in a business called Halo, Purely for Pets, which sells natural pet food and other products—and she gave samples to those in her audience the day the announcement was made. DeGeneres mentioned that she had started to give one of her own dogs the food a few years before when the dog seemed to be allergic to everything.

"One of the things that I really believe is that, if you're going to have pets, you should treat them like you'd treat yourself," she said in a letter on Halo's Web site. "I don't mean you should treat them to new shoes or a fancy car— I'm talking about the basics; a nice bed, fun toys, and good food."[11]

DeGeneres joked with a reporter once that the behavior of animals was more honest than people's behavior. "I'll tell ya," she said, "people are a lot more dangerous. What I've learned is that you've gotta really keep your distance, squat, keep your eyes down like you're eating. Then the network executives don't get you."[12]

Certainly, after many years in show business, DeGeneres has learned how to keep the network executives at bay. One way, of course, is to continue to attract viewers. Indeed, DeGeneres has done that. She came under fire again, briefly in 2007, when she was one of very few talk-show hosts who continued to create new shows during a national strike of television writers. A columnist for *The New York Post* said that the decision could be one that DeGeneres would regret; however, a few months later, when the strike was settled, DeGeneres's show seemed to suffer no harm.[13]

In fact, the popularity of *The Ellen DeGeneres Show* seemed to grow. By early 2008, the Harris Poll announced that DeGeneres topped the list in its annual survey of people's favorite TV stars. In the previous year's poll, DeGeneres had ranked eighth. Oprah Winfrey fell to second place, after five years in the top spot as the poll's favorite television star. Also in the poll, DeGeneres ranked top among single women and those who were of liberal politics.[14]

With her success, DeGeneres became more involved in outside projects. She, along with other celebrities, became part of a national campaign called "The Members Project." Sponsored by American Express, The Members Project is an online initiative focused on making a positive impact on the world. DeGeneres filmed a television commercial for American Express with a tortoise, a giraffe, and penguins that ended up winning an Emmy. It was called "My Life Goal: To Work With Animals." In addition, she launched a series of 32 greeting cards with American Express called "The Ellen Collection."[15]

DeGeneres was doing extremely well, both as a comedian and as a businesswoman. By this point, her talk show had won 25 Daytime Emmy Awards over five seasons, including four for Outstanding Talk Show and four for Outstanding Talk Show Host. By 2008, DeGeneres had also won four People's Choice Awards for Favorite Daytime Talk Show Host, four People's Choice Awards for being the Favorite Funny Female Star, and two Johnny Carson Producer of the Year Awards in Variety Television.

Time magazine readers voted DeGeneres their Favorite TV Host in a competition that had her up against Oprah Winfrey, Kelly Ripa, Regis Philbin, and Meredith Vieira. In addition, *Time* also named her among the 100 Most Influential People in 2006.

A SMALL DOSE OF THE ISSUES

As the 2008 presidential campaign heated up, two major contenders visited DeGeneres's show—just a few days apart in October 2007. Even though she preferred not to be involved in politics, DeGeneres recognized the importance of the presidential primary that was under way. Democratic candidate Hillary Clinton stopped by for the second time during the season to chat with DeGeneres for a bit, and Democrat Barack Obama spent a few minutes dancing onstage when he visited. The visits by Clinton and Obama spoke to DeGeneres's popularity; the candidates knew that she had an audience they needed to reach.

The Republican candidate for president, John McCain, also hoped to appeal to DeGeneres's audience. He visited

Ellen DeGeneres welcomed Republican presidential nominee John McCain to her show in May 2008. Although she usually avoids controversial topics, DeGeneres asked McCain about his stance on gay marriage, which differs from hers. Presidential candidates Hillary Clinton and Barack Obama also were guests on DeGeneres's show.

in May 2008, shortly after the California Supreme Court had overturned a ban on gay marriage. After that ruling, DeGeneres said that she and de Rossi planned to get married. While DeGeneres usually avoided controversial topics on her show, she asked McCain about his thoughts on gay marriage. Although he said that people should be able to enter into legal agreements, he added, "I just believe in the unique status of marriage between man and woman. And I know that we have a respectful disagreement on that issue."

DeGeneres responded: "It just feels like there is this old way of thinking that we are not all the same. We are all the same people, all of us. You're no different than I am. Our love is the same."[16] Although the two disagreed with each other, the exchange was polite and respectful. And DeGeneres injected a dose of humor. At the end, McCain wished her every happiness. To which DeGeneres replied, "So you'll walk me down the aisle?"[17]

With laughter and composure, DeGeneres made her point. A few months later, she and de Rossi did walk down the aisle, as they were married in a very private ceremony on August 16, 2008, at their home in Beverly Hills. Nineteen guests attended, including both of their mothers, Vance, Ellen's father, and other family members. Both wore ensembles created by designer Zac Posen. DeGeneres was dressed in a crisp, white suit, and de Rossi was fitted in a flowing, light pink gown. (In November 2008, in response to the California Supreme Court ruling, voters in that state narrowly approved a ballot measure to ban gay marriage.)

In her own unassuming way, DeGeneres has been making an impact for years. In 2008, *Out* magazine named her the most influential gay woman in America, placing her No. 1 in its "Power 50" issue. When she and her character came out in 1997, gay people cheered to see someone so prominent be a representative of them. And her actions have given countless people the courage to disclose their sexuality.

In the years since then, DeGeneres has perhaps helped many people change their views on homosexuality. In 2005, the University of Minnesota released three studies that showed that exposure to gay television characters reduces prejudice. "Ellen coming out 10 years ago kicked off a tremendous decade of visibility for lesbian, gay, bisexual, and transgendered people," Neil G. Giuliano, the president of the Gay and Lesbian Alliance Against Defamation

(GLAAD), said in 2007. "We know that with this kind of visibility comes understanding and acceptance."[18]

NIFTY AT FIFTY

Still, what DeGeneres wants to do most is entertain. She was continuing to make people laugh—a skill she had honed for more than 35 years since her mother was diagnosed with cancer and DeGeneres made it her job to humor her.

As her fiftieth birthday approached in January 2008, DeGeneres's staff provided a variety of surprises. Her DJ at the time surprised her with a guest appearance from the band Dramarama. As she danced, DeGeneres sang "settle down, settle down, settle down" along with the band. Perhaps turning 50 had DeGeneres contemplating that it was time to settle down and be content with the success that she had sought for her entire adult life. Her struggles as a comedian, it seemed, were over. She had a popular daily talk show and had become a much-acclaimed celebrity. That day, DeGeneres danced around the show as if she didn't have a care in the world.

Along with her success, she has continued to be the thoughtful and caring person she has always been. DeGeneres was still worried about her native New Orleans, and for her birthday she asked fans to contribute to Brad Pitt's Make It Right Project, which had a goal of building 150 houses for displaced residents there. One day on her show, representatives from an ice cream company arrived with a $100,000 check for New Orleans and a big coffee-flavored ice cream cake for DeGeneres's birthday.

On another day, Dr. Wayne Dyer—an author who focuses on self-development—appeared on the show. DeGeneres had been listening to audio versions of his self-help books in her car as she commuted to the studio every day, and she wanted to talk with him in person. "Most of us just are not living the life that we're destined for," Dyer explained. "(We should) be in a place of peace. Be in a place of kindness."[19]

Backstage, Ellen DeGeneres shows off the 2008 Emmy she received as Outstanding Talk Show Host. *The Ellen DeGeneres Show* has won 25 Daytime Emmy Awards in the five seasons it has run.

DeGeneres liked the message she was hearing. "I want to feel good," she responded. "I just feel good when I listen to you in the car. I feel good when I read your words."[20]

Besides the more serious segments, like the one with Dyer, DeGeneres sprinkled plenty of humor in the shows leading up to her birthday. She shared some funny products with the audience—a teddy bear seat-belt holder designed to make seat belts more comfortable and a swirling chair that DeGeneres loved. But her staff members knew what she liked best—on the day before her birthday, which was a Saturday, they brought in a huge red velvet cake and Pinkberry frozen yogurt. In her monologue on this celebratory day, DeGeneres thanked her Mom—who had given birth to her 50 years earlier. Betty DeGeneres beamed from her seat in the audience. One of DeGeneres's best friends, *American Idol* host Ryan Seacrest, showed up for a chat. Videotaped birthday messages were played from dozens of celebrities, including Alicia Keys, Lyle Lovett, Patti LaBelle, Janet Jackson, and Tom Cruise.

"I grew up wanting to make people happy, and it feels good to me," DeGeneres said. "This is just an excuse for a celebration."[21]

Adding even more humor to the show, representatives from the American Association for Retired Persons presented her with an official membership letter. In addition, they presented DeGeneres with a $200,000 check for Brad Pitt's Make It Right Project. (Within a month, contributors from the DeGeneres show had donated nearly $1 million to the project.)

DeGeneres took the birthday celebration as an opportunity to share words of wisdom that a half-century of life had taught her. "I have learned to be comfortable in my own skin," she said. "Don't try to be anything other than who you are. Do what you want to do and don't put it off."[22]

Right after that her DJ started the song: "Get Up Offa That Thing." Of course, DeGeneres and her audience danced!

CHRONOLOGY

1958   Ellen Lee DeGeneres is born on January 26 at Ochsner Foundation Hospital near New Orleans, Louisiana.

1976   Graduates from Atlanta High School in Atlanta, Texas, after moving there with her mother, Betty DeGeneres.

1978   Tells her mother that she is gay.

1984   Is named Showtime's Funniest Person in America.

1986   Makes her first appearance on *The Tonight Show* with Johnny Carson.

1989   Appears as Margo Van Meter in the Fox sitcom *Open House.*

1991   Is named Best Female Stand-Up at the American Comedy Awards.

1992   Appears in *Laurie Hill*, an ABC sitcom.

1994   Appears in *These Friends of Mine* on ABC.

1995   ABC changes the name of *These Friends of Mine* to *Ellen*; DeGeneres publishes her first book, *My Point . . . And I Do Have One.*

1996   Stars in her first feature film, *Mr. Wrong.*

1997   *Ellen* makes television history when the lead character, Ellen Morgan, announces that she is gay in an April episode; DeGeneres begins to talk publicly about being gay; she wins an Emmy Award for Outstanding Writing in a Comedy Series.

1998   ABC cancels *Ellen* because of low ratings and fewer advertisers.

2001   *The Ellen Show*, a sitcom, appears on CBS but is canceled because of low ratings.

2003 DeGeneres launches *The Ellen DeGeneres Show*, a daytime talk show; DeGeneres does the voiceover for a fish named Dory in the movie *Finding Nemo*; DeGeneres's second book, *The Funny Thing Is . . .* , is published.

2004 *The Ellen DeGeneres Show* wins Outstanding Talk Show during the Daytime Emmy Awards.

2005 *The Ellen DeGeneres Show* wins Daytime Emmy Awards for Outstanding Talk Show and Outstanding Talk Show Host.

2006 *The Ellen DeGeneres Show* again wins Daytime Emmys for Outstanding Talk Show and Outstanding Talk Show Host.

2007 *The Ellen DeGeneres Show* again wins Daytime Emmys for Outstanding Talk Show and Outstanding Talk Show Host; DeGeneres is the second woman ever to host the Academy Awards ceremony.

2008 DeGeneres is ranked the new favorite television personality by the Harris Poll, knocking Oprah Winfrey to No. 2 following her five-year hold on the position; DeGeneres wins a Daytime Emmy Award for Outstanding Talk Show Host; she marries actress Portia de Rossi on August 16.

NOTES

CHAPTER 1: SHE'S A DANCING MACHINE

1. "Iggy," *The Ellen DeGeneres Show* Web site. October 16, 2007. Available online at http://ellen.warnerbros.com/2007/10/iggy.php.

2. Evan Henerson, "A Stand-Up Woman: Comedian Ellen DeGeneres Has Taken It Back On the Road," *Chicago Tribune*. July 12, 2000.

3. Harriet Winslow, "Ellen DeGeneres: Comic Gets Help from Her 'Friends'," *The Washington Post*. May 1, 1994.

4. Ellen DeGeneres, "Ellen DeGeneres on Her New Show," *Larry King Live* transcript. September 7, 2004.

5. Ellen DeGeneres, *My Point . . . and I Do Have One*. New York: Bantam Dell, 1995, p. 7.

6. Betty DeGeneres, *Love, Ellen*. New York: William Morrow & Company, 1999, p. 120.

7. Ibid., p. 164.

8. Ibid., p. 4.

9. Julie Lynem, "Stand-Up Is Only Part of DeGeneres' Act," *Detroit Free Press*. June 13, 1993.

10. Ellen DeGeneres, "Ellen DeGeneres on Her New Show."

11. The Associated Press, "Names in the News." August 30, 1984.

12. Henerson, "A Stand-Up Woman."

13. Ellen DeGeneres, "Ellen DeGeneres on Her New Show."

14. Lea Goldman, "TV's Top Earners," *Forbes*. September 27, 2007.

15. Lea Goldman and Kiri Blakeley, "The 20 Richest Women in Entertainment," *Forbes*. January 18, 2007.

16. Bill Carter, "At Lunch With: Ellen DeGeneres; Dialed God (Pause). He Laughed," *The New York Times*. April 13, 1994.

CHAPTER 2: A BROKEN HOME

1. Betty DeGeneres, *Love, Ellen*, p. 70.

2. Ibid., p. 87.

3. Jenny Wilson, "Meet the Moms," *In Style*. May 1, 2004.

4. Julie Jordan and Michelle Tauber, "Ellen at Home, at Ease," *People Weekly*. November 14, 2005.

5. Vance DeGeneres, "TV/Radio Bio." Vance DeGeneres: Official Web site. Available online at http://www.vancedegeneres.com/pages/tv/.

6. Ellen DeGeneres, *My Point . . . and I Do Have One*, p. 3.

7. Ellen DeGeneres, "My Lint Free Thoughts," *The Ellen DeGeneres Show* Web site. January 10, 2008.

8. Carter, "At Lunch With: Ellen DeGeneres."

9. Wilson, "Meet the Moms."

10. "Actresses Ellen DeGeneres, Anne Heche, and Sharon Stone Discuss HBO's Controversial *If These Walls Could Talk 2*," *Larry King Live Weekend* transcript. March 4, 2000.

11. Chandler Rabens, "Ellen Uncensored," *Teen People*. February 2006.

12. Ibid.

13. Ellen DeGeneres, "The First Laugh," *The Ellen DeGeneres Show* Web site. November 8, 2007.

14. Rabens, "Ellen Uncensored."

15. Ellen DeGeneres, "Teenagers," *The Ellen DeGeneres Show* Web site. December 18, 2007.

16. Ellen DeGeneres, "Ellen DeGeneres on Her New Show."

17. Ibid.

18. Ibid.

19. "Wry Toast," *People Weekly*. July 19, 1999.

20. Betty DeGeneres, *Love, Ellen*, p. 4.

21. Allen Johnson, "Two Comedians Take a Look at Their Lives in the Trenches," *Chicago Tribune*. February 7, 1992.

22. "Betty DeGeneres' *Love, Ellen*," from interview transcripts on *Good Morning America*. March 23, 1999.

CHAPTER 3: THE FUNNIEST PERSON IN AMERICA

1. Ellen DeGeneres, "Ellen DeGeneres on Her New Show."

2. Steve Schneider, "Cable TV Notes: Those Fillers Are Doing Double Duty," *The New York Times*. September 2, 1984.

3. Carter, "At Lunch With: Ellen DeGeneres."

4. Debra K. Minor, "Ellen DeGeneres: She's Hip, She's Funny. She's on TV. Just Don't Call Her the Female Seinfeld," *The Buffalo News*. May 14, 1994.

5. The Associated Press, "Names in the News." August 28, 1984.

6. The Associated Press, "Names in the News." August 30, 1984.

7. "AIEF's 'Funny Side' Garners Support for Serious Business," *Adweek*. November 18, 1985.

8. John J. O'Connor, "TV Reviews: 'The Young Comedians' Is Presented on HBO," *The New York Times*. November 26, 1986.

9. Michael Snyder, "Solo 'Rei Momo': Talking Heads' Byrne Takes a Latin Turn," *The San Francisco Chronicle*. October 15, 1989.

10. "Ellen DeGeneres Biography," People.com. Available online at http://www.people.com/people/ellen_degeneres/biography.

11. Allan Johnson, "8 Comics to Tape 'One Night Stands' at the VIC Theatre," *Chicago Tribune*. November 9, 1990.

12. "Ellen DeGeneres Bio," *The Ellen DeGeneres Show* Web site. Available online at http://ellen.warnerbros.com/about/bio.php.

13. Charles Leerhsen, "Women Who Kill—Nightly," *Newsweek*. June 15, 1992.

14. Susie Linfield, "Wisecracks," *San Francisco Chronicle*. October 11, 1992.

15. Ibid.

16. Lawrence Toppman, "Ellen DeGeneres' Humor Is in a Class by Itself," *The Buffalo News*. August 17, 1991.

17. Allan Johnson, "8 Comics to Tape 'One Night Stands' at the VIC Theatre."

CHAPTER 4: A TELEVISION STAR

1. Jim Santella, "With Razor-Sharp Wit and PG Humor, Ellen DeGeneres Is Controlled Chaos," *The Buffalo News*. June 9, 1994.

2. Carter, "At Lunch With: Ellen DeGeneres."

3. Winslow, "Comic Gets Help From Her 'Friends'."

4. Colin Covert, "With a Little Help from Her 'Friends'," *Star-Tribune*. May 13, 1994.

5. Lynem, "Stand-Up Is Only Part of DeGeneres' Act."

6. Carter, "At Lunch With: Ellen DeGeneres."

7. Allan Johnson, "For Laughs, 2 Ellens Are Better Than 1," *Chicago Tribune*. May 23, 1994.

8. Carter, "At Lunch With: Ellen DeGeneres."

9.   Tom Green, "A Stand-Up Standout/A DeGeneres Helping of New Attention," *USA Today*. September 21, 1994.

10.   Minor, "Ellen DeGeneres: She's Hip."

11.   Rene Rodriguez, "Wrong Isn't Right for DeGeneres," *The Miami Herald*. February 20, 1996.

12.   "Prime Times: Suddenly Even the Emmys Have Attitude," *People Weekly*. September 25, 1995.

13.   "Gucci at Goldie's: Hollywood's Buy-at-Lunch Bunch Gives for Charity—and Gets a Good Discount," *People Weekly*. July 1, 1996.

14.   Frank Ahrens, "DeGeneres: Her Roots Are Showing," *The Washington Post*. May 17, 2000.

15.   "Viva Vegas! The First Hard Rock Hotel Opens, Dense with Celebs," *People Weekly*. March 27, 1995.

16.   Mike Duffy, "Ellen DeGeneres Finds TV Gossip Hard to Take," *Lexington Herald-Leader*. January 14, 1996.

17.   Kathleen Rizzo Young, "Ellen DeGeneres to a Fault," *The Buffalo News*. September 17, 1995.

18.   Rick Marin and Sue Miller, "Ellen Steps Out," *Newsweek*. April 14, 1997.

19.   Lynn Elber, "DeGeneres' Sitcom Gets New Name, New Time Slot at ABC," *Chicago Tribune*. August 6, 1994.

20.   Alan Pergament, "Same Ellen, But Lots of New and Different Things on *Ellen*," *The Buffalo News*. August 2, 1994.

21.   James Endrst, "Ellen DeGeneres Adjusts to Life in the Glare of TV's Spotlight," *Pittsburgh Post-Gazette*. August 28, 1994.

22.   Ibid.

23.   Minor, "Ellen DeGeneres: She's Hip."

24.   Jackie Hyman, "No More Delays or Disasters: DeGeneres Finally Gets a Break," *Chicago Tribune*. March 26, 1994.

25.   Duffy, "Ellen DeGeneres Finds TV Gossip Hard to Take."

26.   Alan Pergament, "Ellen's On the Defensive and Feeling Awkward," *The Buffalo News*. January 17, 1996.

27.   Ibid.

28.   "DeGeneres to Serve as MC of Grammys," *Chicago Tribune*. January 31, 1996.

29. Ginia Bellafante, "Looking for An Out: Is Ellen Gay? A Controversy over Sexuality Is the Least of this Muddled Sitcom's Problems," *Time*. October 7, 1996.

CHAPTER 5: LIFE CHANGES

1. Bellafante, "Looking for An Out."
2. Ibid.
3. Sharon Krum, "Women: She's Out with the In-Crowd," *The Guardian* (London). December 17, 1996.
4. "Ellen 'Willing to Take Risk,' but Will She Do It?" *The Miami Herald*. October 23, 1996.
5. Tom Gliatto, "Picks and Pans," *People Weekly*. November 25, 1996.
6. Marin and Miller, "Ellen Steps Out."
7. Bruce Handy, "Roll Over, Ward Cleaver," *Time*. April 14, 1997.
8. Ibid.
9. Bruce Handy, "He Called Me Ellen DeGenerate?" *Time*. April 14, 1997.
10. Marin and Miller, "Ellen Steps Out."
11. Handy, "Roll Over, Ward Cleaver."
12. Marin and Miller, "Ellen Steps Out."
13. Ibid.
14. Handy, "Roll Over, Ward Cleaver."
15. Betty DeGeneres, *Love, Ellen*, pp. 143–145.
16. Marin and Miller, "Ellen Steps Out."
17. Ellen DeGeneres' Family Speaks Out." *PrimeTime*. April 30, 1997. Available online at http://vanceypantsdegeneres.tripod.com/witeout/1997primetime.htm.
18. Ibid.
19. Ibid.
20. "DeGeneres Mom Urges Coming Out," Associated Press Online. September 9, 1997.
21. "Speaking Out," *People Weekly*. September 15, 1997.
22. "History of National Coming Out Day: 1997: Super Mom." Human Rights Campaign Web site. Available online at http://www.hrc.org/issues/3367.htm.

23. John Leo, "Why Ruin a Good Story," *U.S. News & World Report*. May 5, 1997.

24. Betty DeGeneres, *Love, Ellen*, p. 271.

25. William Saletan, "The Gay Fray," *Slate*. November 16, 1997.

CHAPTER 6: ANOTHER CHANCE

1. Joshua Hammer, "Ellen: Gaying, Gaying, Gone." *Newsweek*. March 23, 1998.

2. Ibid.

3. Richard Huff, "DeGeneres Predicts ABC Will Cancel 'Ellen' Because of Her Homosexuality," *Daily News* (New York). February 24, 1998.

4. Howard Cohen, "DeGeneres Off Her Soapbox and Back to Stand-Up," *Chicago Tribune*. June 27, 2000.

5. Kate Aurthur, "Cry Me a River," *Slate*. December 4, 1998.

6. Michael Posner, "It's Just Ellen, a Stand-Up Gal," *The Globe and Mail*. May 1, 2002.

7. Cohen, "DeGeneres Off Her Soapbox and Back to Stand-Up."

8. Henerson, "A Stand-Up Woman."

9. Ibid.

10. *Ellen DeGeneres: The Beginning*, 2000.

11. Ibid.

12. Allan Johnson, "DeGeneres Plays It as Sharp as Ever," *Chicago Tribune*. May 22, 2000.

13. Jeffrey Ressner, "10 Questions for Ellen DeGeneres," *Time*. February 23, 2004.

14. Tom Shales, "Walls 2: A Window into Women's Hearts," *The Washington Post*. March 4, 2000.

15. "Actresses Ellen DeGeneres, Anne Heche, and Sharon Stone Discuss HBO's Controversial *If These Walls Could Talk 2*," *Larry King Live Weekend* transcripts. March 4, 2000.

16. Ellen DeGeneres, "Ellen DeGeneres on Her New Show."

17. Posner, "It's Just Ellen, a Stand-Up Gal."

18. Ellen DeGeneres, "Ellen DeGeneres on Her New Show."

19. Alan Pergament, "Ellen DeGeneres Hits Home Run with Just the Right Tone as Emmy Host," *The Buffalo News*. November 5, 2001.

20. Cohen, "DeGeneres Off Her Soapbox and Back to Stand-Up."
21. *"New York Times* Bestselling Author Ellen DeGeneres to Publish New Book of Comic Essays with Simon & Schuster." PR Newswire. August 12, 2002.
22. Nicolas Fonseca, "The New Queen of Nice," *Entertainment Weekly*. September 12, 2003.
23. Ibid.
24. Louis B. Hobson, "Ellen DeGeneres Has a Whale of a Time Acting as a Fish in *Finding Nemo*," *Toronto Sun*. May 25, 2003.
25. Fonseca, "The New Queen of Nice."
26. Ibid.

CHAPTER 7: MOVIN' AND GROOVIN' ON TV

1. Ibid.
2. Ibid.
3. Posner, "It's Just Ellen, a Stand-Up Gal."
4. Ressner, "10 Questions for Ellen DeGeneres."
5. Fonseca, "The New Queen of Nice."
6. Ibid.
7. "Ellen DeGeneres Discusses Her New Talk Show, *The Ellen DeGeneres Show*, Premiering Today," NBC News transcripts for *Today*. September 8, 2003.
8. Ibid.
9. Ellen DeGeneres, "Ellen DeGeneres on Her New Show."
10. Fonseca, "The New Queen of Nice."
11. "Ellen DeGeneres Discusses Her New Talk Show, *The Ellen DeGeneres Show*, Premiering Today," NBC News transcripts for *Today*.
12. Ibid.
13. Fonseca, "The New Queen of Nice."
14. "Ellen DeGeneres Discusses Her New Talk Show and Book," National Public Radio *Weekend Edition* transcripts. December 13, 2003.
15. Jordan and Tauber, "Ellen at Home, at Ease."
16. Ellen DeGeneres, "Ellen DeGeneres on Her New Show."
17. Jordan and Tauber, "Ellen at Home, at Ease."

18. Bob Newhart, "Ellen DeGeneres," *Time*. April 30, 2006.
19. Jordan and Tauber, "Ellen at Home, at Ease."
20. Ibid.
21. Richard Huff, "A Very Tough Act to Follow," *Daily News* (New York). September 2, 2005.
22. Jordan and Tauber, "Ellen at Home, at Ease."
23. Ellen DeGeneres, "Ellen DeGeneres on Her New Show."
24. *Today*, from transcripts found in BurrellesLuce Information Services. November 21, 2005.
25. Ibid.
26. Ibid.
27. Ibid.
28. James Patrick Herman, "TV's Funniest Chat Queen Talks Up a Few of Her Favorite Things," *In Style*. April 1, 2005.
29. DeGeneres, Ellen, "Ellen DeGeneres Discusses Her Personal Ties to New Orleans," *The Saturday Morning Early Show* transcripts. September 3, 2005.
30. Ibid.
31. "Ellen DeGeneres Biography," People.com. Available online at http://www.people.com/people/ellen_degeneres/biography/.
32. "The Ellen DeGeneres Show and Quiznos Make the American Dream Come True," Business Wire. January 26, 2006.
33. Stacey Plaisance, "DeGeneres Visits New Orleans for First Time Since Katrina," The Associated Press. May 12, 2006.
34. Ibid.
35. Arthur Nead, "Commencement 2006," Tulane University. Available online at http://www2.tulane.edu/article_news_details.cfm?ArticleID=6744.
36. Ibid.
37. Ibid.

CHAPTER 8: MORE THAN A COMEDIAN

1. "Oscar Night: Host Ellen DeGeneres," available online at http://www.oscar.com.
2. Ibid.
3. Ibid.

4. Dan Snierson, "Hostess Treat," *Entertainment Weekly*. February 2, 2007.

5. James Poniewozik, "Yep, She's Mainstream," *Time*. March 5, 2007.

6. "Interview With: Melissa Etheridge," available online at http://www.oscars.com.

7. David Ansen, "Analyzing Oscar: A Kodak Moment for Ellen and Marty," *Newsweek*. February 26, 2007.

8. "Iggy," *The Ellen DeGeneres Show* Web site. October 16, 2007. Available online at http://ellen.warnerbros.com/2007/10/iggy.php.

9. Emil Steiner, "Cry Me a River, Ellen DeGeneres," *The Washington Post*. October 17, 2007.

10. Ellen DeGeneres, "So You Think You Can Dance?" *The Ellen DeGeneres Show* Web site. November 8, 2007.

11. "Letter from Ellen DeGeneres," Halo, Purely for Pets Web site.

12. Covert, "With a Little Help from Her 'Friends'."

13. Richard Johnson, "Strikebreaker Ellen Blasted," *New York Post*. November 9, 2007.

14. "Ellen DeGeneres Is New Favorite TV Personality as Oprah Slips to Number Two," The Harris Poll Web site. January 14, 2008.

15. "Ellen DeGeneres Bio," *The Ellen DeGeneres Show* Web site. Available online at http://ellen.warnerbros.com/about/bio.php.

16. Michael Y. Park, "McCain Clashes with DeGeneres on Gay Marriage," People.com. May 22, 2008.

17. Mark Silva, "Ellen DeGeneres Weds: McCain Walking Me?" *Chicago Tribune*. May 22, 2008.

18. "Ellen: 10 Years Out," Gay and Lesbian Alliance Against Defamation Web site. April 10, 2007.

19. *The Ellen DeGeneres Show*, January 24, 2008.

20. Ibid.

21. *The Ellen DeGeneres Show*, January 25, 2008.

22. Ibid.

BIBLIOGRAPHY

"Actresses Ellen DeGeneres, Anne Heche, and Sharon Stone Discuss HBO's Controversial *If These Walls Could Talk 2*." *Larry King Live Weekend* transcript. March 4, 2000.

Ahrens, Frank. "DeGeneres: Her Roots Are Showing." *Washington Post*. May 17, 2000.

"AIEF's 'Funny Side' Garners Support for Serious Business." *Adweek*. November 18, 1985.

Ansen, David. "Analyzing Oscar: A Kodak Moment for Ellen and Marty." *Newsweek*. February 26, 2007.

Aurthur, Kate. "Cry Me a River." *Slate*. December 4, 1998.

Bellafante, Ginia. "Looking for an Out: Is Ellen Gay? A Controversy over Sexuality Is the Least of this Muddled Sitcom's Problems." *Time*. October 7, 1996.

Carter, Bill. "At Lunch With: Ellen DeGeneres; Dialed God (Pause). He Laughed." *New York Times*. April 13, 1994.

Cohen, Howard. "DeGeneres Off Her Soapbox and Back to Stand-Up." *Chicago Tribune*. June 27, 2000.

Covert, Colin. "With a Little Help from Her 'Friends.'" *Star-Tribune*. May 13, 1994.

DeGeneres, Betty. *Love, Ellen*. New York: William Morrow & Company, 1999.

DeGeneres, Ellen. "Ellen DeGeneres on Her New Show." *Larry King Live* transcript. September 7, 2004.

———. "My Lint Free Thoughts." *The Ellen DeGeneres Show* Web site. January 10, 2008.

———. *My Point . . . and I Do Have One*, New York: Bantam Dell, 1995.

———. "Teenagers." *The Ellen DeGeneres Show* Web site. December 18, 2007.

———. "The First Laugh." *The Ellen DeGeneres Show* Web site. November 8, 2007.

———. "Ellen DeGeneres Discusses Her Personal Ties to New Orleans." *The Saturday Morning Early Show* transcripts. September 3, 2005.

"DeGeneres Mom Urges Coming Out." Associated Press Online. September 9, 1997.

"DeGeneres to Serve as MC of Grammys." *Chicago Tribune*. January 31, 1996.

Due, Tananarive. "Need a Laugh? HBO Show Brings Comedy Crew to Town for Week of One-Liners." *Miami Herald*. March 10, 1992.

Duffy, Mike. "Ellen DeGeneres Finds TV Gossip Hard to Take." *Lexington Herald-Leader*. January 14, 1996.

Elber, Lynn. "DeGeneres' Sitcom Gets New Name, New Time Slot at ABC." *Chicago Tribune*. August 6, 1994.

"Ellen DeGeneres Bio." *The Ellen DeGeneres Show* Web site. Available online at http://ellen.warnerbros.com/about/bio.php.

"Ellen DeGeneres Biography." People.com. Available online at http://www.people.com/people/ellen_degeneres/biography.

"Ellen DeGeneres Discusses Her New Talk Show and Book." National Public Radio *Weekend Edition* transcripts. December 13, 2003.

"Ellen DeGeneres Discusses Her New Talk Show, *The Ellen DeGeneres Show*, Premiering Today." NBC News transcripts. September 8, 2003.

"Ellen DeGeneres' Family Speaks Out." *PrimeTime*. Available online at http://vanceypantsdegeneres.tripod.com/witeout/1997primetime.htm. April 30, 1997.

"Ellen DeGeneres Is New Favorite TV Personality as Oprah Slips to Number Two." The Harris Poll Web site. January 14, 2008.

"Ellen: 10 Years Out." Gay and Lesbian Alliance Against Defamation Web site. April 10, 2007.

"Ellen 'Willing to Take Risk,' but Will She Do It?" *Miami Herald*. October 23, 1996.

Endrst, James. "Ellen DeGeneres Adjusts to Life in the Glare of TV's Spotlight." *Pittsburgh Post-Gazette*. August 28, 1994.

Fonseca, Nicholas. "The New Queen of Nice." *Entertainment Weekly*. September 12, 2003.

Gliatto, Tom. "Picks and Pans." *People Weekly*. November 25, 1996.

Goldman, Lea. "TV's Top Earners." *Forbes*. September 27, 2007.

Goldman, Lea, and Kiri Blakeley. "The 20 Richest Women in Entertainment." *Forbes*. January 18, 2007.

Green, Tom. "A Stand-Up Standout/A DeGeneres Helping of New Attention." *USA Today*. September 21, 1994.

"Gucci at Goldie's: Hollywood's Buy-at-Lunch Bunch Gives for Charity—and Gets a Good Discount." *People Weekly*. July 1, 1996.

Hammer, Joshua. "Ellen: Gaying, Gaying, Gone." *Newsweek*. March 23, 1998.

Handy, Bruce. "Roll Over, Ward Cleaver." *Time*. April 14, 1997.

———. "He Called Me Ellen DeGenerate?" *Time*. April 14, 1997.

Henerson, Evan. "A Stand-Up Woman: Comedian Ellen DeGeneres Has Taken It Back On the Road." *Chicago Tribune*. July 12, 2000.

Herman, James Patrick. "TV's Funniest Chat Queen Talks Up a Few of Her Favorite Things." *In Style*. April 1, 2005.

"History of National Coming Out Day: 1997: Super Mom." Human Rights Campaign Web site. Available online at http://www.hrc.org/issues/3367.htm.

Hobson, Louis B. "Ellen DeGeneres Has a Whale of a Time Acting As a Fish in *Finding Nemo*." *Toronto Sun*. May 25, 2003.

Huff, Richard. "A Very Tough Act to Follow." *Daily News* (New York). September 2, 2005.

———. "DeGeneres Predicts ABC Will Cancel 'Ellen' Because of Her Homosexuality." *Daily News* (New York). February 24, 1998.

Hyman, Jackie. "No More Delays or Disasters: DeGeneres Finally Gets a Break." *Chicago Tribune*. March 26, 1994.

"Iggy." *The Ellen DeGeneres Show* Web site. October 16, 2007. Available online at http://ellen.warnerbros.com/2007/10/iggy.php.

"Interview With: Melissa Etheridge." Available online at www.oscars.org.

Johnson, Allan. "8 Comics to Tape 'One Night Stands' at the VIC Theatre." *Chicago Tribune*. November 9, 1990.

———. "Two Comedians Take a Look at Their Lives in the Trenches." *Chicago Tribune*. February 7, 1992.

———. "For Laughs, 2 Ellens Are Better Than 1." *Chicago Tribune*. May 23, 1994.

———. "DeGeneres Plays It As Sharp As Ever." *Chicago Tribune*. May 22, 2000.

Johnson, Richard. "Strikebreaker Ellen Blasted." *New York Post*. November 9, 2007.

Jordan, Julie, and Michelle Tauber. "Ellen at Home, at Ease." *People Weekly*. November 14, 2005.

Krum, Sharon. "Women: She's Out with the In-Crowd." *The Guardian*. December 17, 1996.

Leerhsen, Charles. "Women Who Kill—Nightly." *Newsweek*. June 15, 1992.

Leo, John. "Why Ruin a Good Story?" *U.S. News & World Report*. May 5, 1997.

Linfield, Susie. "Wisecracks." *San Francisco Chronicle*. October 11, 1992.

Lynem, Julie. "Stand-Up Is Only Part of DeGeneres' Act." *Detroit Free Press*. June 13, 1993.

Marin, Rick, and Sue Miller. "Ellen Steps Out." *Newsweek*. April 14, 1997.

Minor, Debra K. "Ellen DeGeneres: She's Hip, She's Funny. She's on TV. Just Don't Call Her the Female Seinfeld." *Buffalo News*. May 14, 1994.

"Names in the News." The Associated Press. August 28, 1984.

Nead, Arthur. "Commencement 2006." Tulane University. Available online at http://www2.tulane.edu/article_news_details. cfm?ArticleID=6744

"*New York Times* Bestselling Author Ellen DeGeneres to Publish New Book of Comic Essays with Simon & Schuster." PR Newswire. August 12, 2002.

O'Connor, John J. "TV Reviews: 'The Young Comedians' Is Presented on HBO." *New York Times*. November 26, 1986.

Newhart, Bob. "Ellen DeGeneres." *Time*. April 30, 2006.

"Oscar Night: Host Ellen DeGeneres." Available online at http://www. oscar.com.

Paprocki, Sherry. *Black Americans of Achievement: Oprah Winfrey, Talk Show Host and Media Magnate*. New York: Infobase Publishing, 2006.

Park, Michael Y. "McCain Clashes with DeGeneres on Gay Marriage." People.com. May 22, 2008.

Pergament, Alan. "Same Ellen, But Lots of New and Different Things on *Ellen*." *Buffalo News*. August 2, 1994.

Plaisance, Stacey. "DeGeneres Visits New Orleans for First Time Since Katrina." The Associated Press. May 12, 2006.

Poniewozik, James. "Yep, She's Mainstream." *Time*. March 5, 2007.

Posner, Michael. "It's Just Ellen, a Stand-Up Gal." *The Globe and Mail*. May 1, 2002.

"Prime Times: Suddenly Even the Emmys Have Attitude." *People Weekly*. September 25, 1995.

Rabens, Chandler. "Ellen Uncensored." *Teen People*. February 2006.

Ressner, Jeffrey. "10 Questions for Ellen DeGeneres." *Time*. February 23, 2004.

Rodriguez, Rene. "Wrong Isn't Right for DeGeneres." *Miami Herald*. February 20, 1996.

Rose, Lacey. "The Top-Earning Comedians." *Forbes*. October 11, 2007.

Santella, Jim. "With Razor-Sharp Wit and PG Humor, Ellen DeGeneres Is Controlled Chaos." *Buffalo News*. June 9, 1994.

Saletan, William. "The Gay Fray." *Slate*. November 16, 1997.

Schneider, Steve. "Cable TV Notes: Those Fillers Are Doing Double Duty." *New York Times*. September 2, 1984.

Shales, Tom. "Walls 2: A Window Into Women's Hearts." *The Washington Post*. March 4, 2000.

Silva, Mark. "Ellen DeGeneres Weds: McCain Walking Me?" *Chicago Tribune*. May 22, 2008.

Snierson, Dan. "Hostess Treat." *Entertainment Weekly*. February 2, 2007.

Snyder, Michael. "Solo 'Rei Momo': Talking Heads' Byrne Takes a Latin Turn." *San Francisco Chronicle*. October 15, 1989.

"Speaking Out." *People Weekly*. September 15, 1997.

Steiner, Emil. "Cry Me a River, Ellen DeGeneres." *Washington* Post. October 17, 2007.

"The Ellen DeGeneres Show and Quiznos Make the American Dream Come True." Business Wire. January 26, 2006.

Today, from transcripts found in BurrellesLuce Information Services. May 20, 2005.

Today, from transcripts found in BurrellesLuce Information Services. November 21, 2005.

Toppman, Lawrence. "Ellen DeGeneres' Humor Is in a Class by Itself." *Buffalo News*. August 17, 1991.

"TV/Radio Bio." Vance DeGeneres: Official Web site. Available online at http://www.vancedegeneres.com/pages/tv/.

"Viva Vegas! The First Hard Rock Hotel Opens, Dense with Celebs." *People Weekly*. March 27, 1995.

Wilson, Jenny. "Meet the Moms." *In Style*. May 1, 2004.

Winslow, Harriet. "Ellen DeGeneres: Comic Gets Help from Her 'Friends'." *Washington Post*. May 1, 1994.

"Wry Toast." *People Weekly*. July 19, 1999.

Young, Kathleen Rizzo. "Ellen DeGeneres to a Fault." *Buffalo News*. September 17, 1995.

FURTHER RESOURCES

BOOKS

DeGeneres, Betty. *Love, Ellen: A Mother/Daughter Journey*, New York: William Morrow and Company, Inc., 1995.

DeGeneres, Ellen. *My Point . . . and I Do Have One*, New York: Bantam Dell, 1995.

———. *The Funny Thing Is . . .* , New York: Simon & Schuster, 2004.

Irwin, William. *Seinfeld and Philosophy: A Book about Everything and Nothing*, Chicago: Open Court Publishing, 1999.

Leno, Jay. *How to Be the Funniest Kid in the Whole Wide World (Or Just in Your Class)*, New York: Simon & Schuster, 2007.

Mentzel-Gerris, Sharon. *Careers in Comedy*, New York: Rosen Publishing Group, 1993.

Stewart, Gail B. *Great Women Comedians*. San Diego, Calif.: Lucent Books, 2002.

WEB SITES

Celebrity Central: Ellen DeGeneres
http://www.people.com/people/ellen_degeneres

The Ellen DeGeneres Show
http://ellen.warnerbros.com

Human Rights Campaign
http://www.hrc.org

Make It Right Foundation
http://www.makeitrightnola.org/

INDEX

ABOUT THE AUTHOR

SHERRY BECK PAPROCKI has written or contributed to eight books for children. *Oprah Winfrey, Talk Show Host and Media Magnate* (Infobase Publishing, 2006) earned a spot on the 2006 Nonfiction Honor List created by the Voice of Youth Advocates (VOYA). In addition, she has written *Bob Marley, Musician* (Infobase Publishing, 2006); *Vicente Fox* (Chelsea House, 2002); *Katie Couric* (Chelsea House, 2001); and *Michelle Kwan* (Chelsea House, 2001). Her bylines have appeared in *Preservation* magazine, the *Chicago Tribune*, *The Plain Dealer*, *The Philadelphia Inquirer*, the Los Angeles Times Syndicate, and many other publications. She is a graduate of the Ohio State University School of Journalism and resides near Columbus, Ohio, where she also serves as an adjunct faculty member of Otterbein College. She and her husband, Ray, are the parents of two adult children—Justin and Ana Paprocki.

PICTURE CREDITS

Page

8: AP Images
16: AP Images
20: AP Images
25: AP Images
33: Photofest
37: Fox/Photofest
46: AP Images
49: Buena Vista Pictures/ Photofest
53: ABC/Photofest
59: Time & Life Pictures/ Getty Images

63: ABC/Photofest
68: AP Images
74: © John Atashian/Corbis
78: AP Images
85: Telepictures/Photofest
91: AP Images
95: AP Images
101: AP Images
108: AP Images
111: AP Images